THE BYZANTINE WORLD

History

Editor
PROFESSOR JOEL HURSTFIELD
D.LIT
Astor Professor of English History
in the University of London

THE BYZANTINE WORLD

J. M. Hussey
Professor of History
in the University of London

HUTCHINSON UNIVERSITY LIBRARY
LONDON

HUTCHINSON & CO *(Publishers)* LTD
178–202 Great Portland Street, London W1

London Melbourne Sydney
Auckland Bombay Toronto
Johannesburg New York

First published 1957
Second edition 1961
Third (revised) edition 1967
Fourth edition 1970

Cover design of paperback edition shows a floor mosaic
from the Great Palace in Constantinople, probably sixth-
century: detail of mule throwing off rider and bundle of
sticks

© new material J. M. Hussey 1961, 1967 and 1970

Printed in Great Britain by litho on smooth wove paper
by Anchor Press, and bound by Wm. Brendon,
both of Tiptree, Essex

09 022693 3 (cased)
09 022694 1 (paper)

To
N. H. B.

CONTENTS

PREFACE

Byzantium was the name of the old Greek colony on the site that was later to become the City of Constantine and the word was used many centuries later to describe what was supposed to be a declining and decadent medieval Roman Empire. J. B. Bury objected to this and preferred to speak of the 'Eastern Roman Empire'. He used the term 'Eastern' to distinguish this polity with Constantinople as its capital from the medieval 'Western' Empire, and he retained the word 'Roman' because he considered that in essence it was still the Roman Empire. But however strong its links with its Graeco-Roman past, it acquired its own distinctive characteristics, and it is convenient to use the words 'Byzantine' and 'Byzantium' which no longer imply reproach. Scholars during the last fifty years or so, building on the foundations laid by the sixteenth- and seventeenth-century pioneers, of whom Du Cange was outstanding, have enabled us to view the history and civilisation of the Eastern Roman Empire more objectively, to perceive something of its creative achievement and to realise the extent to which its near neighbours, and others further afield, were indebted to it. Historians are beginning to free themselves from the spell of Gibbon. However much they delight in *The Decline and Fall*, they realise that the story of the Byzantine Empire is neither 'uniform' nor 'tedious', as Gibbon thought.

I gratefully acknowledge my debt to Byzantinists past and present, and especially to Professor Norman Baynes who has been an inspiring guide in exploring the world of East Rome and to whom this little book is dedicated in affection and gratitude.

April 1957   J.M.H.

I

THE BYZANTINE EMPIRE TAKES SHAPE

324–717

I. CONSTANTINE THE GREAT AND THE EMERGENCE OF A CHRISTIAN ROMAN EMPIRE

In 324 Byzantium, the old Greek settlement in the triangle of land bordered by the waters of the Golden Horn, the Bosphorus and the Sea of Marmora, was chosen by the Roman Emperor Constantine the Great as the site for a new city to be the headquarters of the Empire in the East. It was formally inaugurated in May 330 as the City of Constantine, his residence and one of the capitals. Various eastern centres had previously been tried out but this proved permanent and was indeed, by its geographical situation, admirably suited to serve as a link between Europe and Asia, between the Black Sea with its unexploited hinterland and the Aegean and Mediterranean Seas opening on the routes to the Middle and Far East. The very foundation of an eastern capital, the seat of the senior Emperor, pointed the way to the middle ages when it was the eastern half of the Roman Empire which survived without any break in its history. It is immaterial whether it is called early Byzantine or late Roman during this formative period inaugurated by Constantine the Great. It was essentially the Roman Empire and as such its culture was predominantly Greek, though with strong oriental influences. This was true of the Roman Empire in the days of St Paul as in the days of St Ambrose. The difference between the world of Paul of Tarsus and of Ambrose of Milan lay however not in the structure of the imperial framework or the nature of Graeco-Roman civilisation, but in two fundamental changes. Internally, increasing concern with the East and with its creeds was symbolised by the New Rome

which rose on the shores of the Bosphorus, the city of the first
Christian Emperor. Externally, the dangerous pressure of a rival
Empire in Persia and the even more threatening menace of migratory
tribes from the North weakened imperial resources, and though
warded off in the East, eventually brought about the political disruption of the western half of the Roman Empire and the rise of
new independent principalities under the control of the Germanic
invaders.

In Constantine the Great's day the imminent disruption of the
western half of the Roman Empire was however not yet apparent.
What must have caused some stir was the Emperor's announcement
of his adoption of Christianity and the toleration and favour hence-
forth accorded the Christian Church, a toleration which by the end
of the fourth century had been replaced by its recognition as the one
true faith and the consequent proscription of all other religions.
Pagan practices were by no means thus eliminated and lingered on
for many generations and even centuries, but it was useless to plead
for toleration or to claim that not by one road alone could so great
a truth be reached. Whatever the nature of the 'conversion' which
Constantine experienced, his belief in the Christian God and his
Roman heritage convinced him of his duty to take the lead in promoting doctrinal and disciplinary unity within the Christian Church.
He called and presided over the first General Council of the Church
at Nicaea (325). He thus personified the close understanding between
Church and State which marked the medieval East Roman Empire.
His historian, Bishop Eusebius, laid the foundations of a theory of
Christian sovereignty, emphasising, not the cleavage between the
two cities or between what was God's and what was Caesar's, but
the Christian Empire, temporal it is true, but sanctified as a divine
instrument and ruled over by an Emperor who was Christ's vice-
gerent on earth. The titles of 'thirteenth apostle' and 'the equal of the
apostles' fitly recognise the place of Constantine the Great in the
medieval polity.

In many respects the Empire in the fourth century shows no
abrupt break with the earlier period; it might just as well be called
late Roman as early Byzantine. It showed its close cultural affinities
with the Hellenistic world, and the adoption of Christianity did not
mean the rejection of pagan civilisation: the learning, art, philosophy
of Greece remained the prized possessions of a Christian Byzantium.
Its government was in essence that of the Graeco-Roman Empire.
It continued to be ruled by a single absolute monarch, whose
authority was enhanced by his special position as the chosen repre-

sentative of the Christian God. Its administration and civil service
were the fruit of long experience, and overhauled by Diocletian and
Constantine provided the machinery of government which formed
the basis of future development, ensuring both continuity and effective central control. The territorial extent of the Empire made it
imperative to give special attention to provincial arrangements. By
the end of the fourth century there were four prefectures: the prefecture of the East (including Egypt, Asia Minor and Thrace), that
of Illyricum (including the central Balkans and Greece), the Italian
prefecture (Italy, the northern Balkans with Dalmatia, and part of
Africa), and that of the Gauls (Britain, Gaul, Spain and W. Maure-
tania). Within these vast areas there was further subdivision into
dioceses and again into provinces. Italy no longer had any special
position. The power of the pretorian prefects was curbed at every
turn. They had only civil authority from Constantine's time on-
ward; Constantinople and Rome were withdrawn from their administration and governed by their own city eparchs; their control
over central governmental departments was curbed by the rise of
rival officials, as the Master of Offices. This diminution of the power
of the pretorian prefects was only one aspect of the constant change
and adaptation of the Roman administrative system. There was
similar flexibility and reorganisation in the military sphere. In the
provinces civil and military authority was no longer vested in the
same man. The *dux* had military control, perhaps over a group of
provinces. The Empire was strengthened, partly by increasing its
frontier defences, especially the border troops who often held their
land in return for military service, and partly by creating a mobile
force which could be used against invaders at any point on the long
frontiers, or employed if need arose against rival claimants to the
throne.

  Military need was indeed the keynote of the early Byzantine state.
The army, itself often recruited and officered by Germanic elements,
was continually called upon to drive back the barbarians on the
north, or to face pressure on the east from the vigorous Persian King
of kings. It was partly because the Danube and the eastern frontiers
were obvious danger spots that Constantine (like Diocletian before
him) had chosen to take over the eastern half of the Empire himself,
while his colleague[1] ruled in the West. The weight of the Empire was
in the East: the *pars orientalis* was wealthier with greater economic
resources, more densely populated, the home of fertile intellectual
and religious activity, and its great cities, such as the cosmopolitan

  1. A co-Emperor of this kind was the normal practice; see pp. 33f. and 82.

Alexandria or Antioch, or even the newly founded but rapidly growing imperial city on the Bosphorus, could rival Rome.

2. THE BARBARIAN INVASIONS AND THE SURVIVAL OF THE EASTERN HALF OF THE EMPIRE

In the late third and throughout the fourth centuries various methods of ruling the Empire were tried, ranging from control by a single Emperor alone to the more elaborate government by four which Diocletian devised. Though there might be one or more assistant Emperors it was emphasised that the Empire remained one and indivisible. All the same the eastern and western halves were growing apart and had different political problems.

In 395, the Emperor Theodosius the Great died and left the eastern half to Arcadius his elder son, the western to the younger Honorius. The indivisibility of the Empire was still maintained. For instance, laws issued for one half were valid if proclaimed in the other half. But political events shattered Roman rule in the West. From the end of the fourth century up to Justinian's reign in the mid-sixth century the West (i.e. the prefectures of Italy and the Gauls) lacked capable Emperors. Collapse in the face of barbarian pressure was averted only by the ability of the generals who took control, themselves often of Germanic origin, such as Stilicho or Ricimer.

The Germanic migratory tribes had long caused grave anxiety to the Empire and were shortly to transform the western provinces from distant Britain to Italy and North Africa. Nor did the East escape unscathed. In the late fourth century the Goths who had been harassing the frontiers poured into the Balkans and crushingly defeated the Roman army in 378. Theodosius the Great and later Emperors tried to deal with this problem in various ways. Many of the Goths settled in the Balkans and were recognised as a kind of military auxiliary force (*foederati*) in the pay of the Emperor, a costly proceeding. They proved a disturbing element, plundering the Balkans and Greece at will and influencing politics, so that the government in Constantinople was only too relieved when they were diverted elsewhere. The Visigoths after sacking Rome in 410 passed to South France and Spain. Later in the century the Emperor Zeno was thankful to send a substantial number of them to Italy, where they went in 488, men, women and children, under the leadership of Theodoric the Ostrogoth.

Italy by the end of the fifth century, like most of the western provinces, was virtually lost to the Empire. The line of Roman

Emperors, the descendants of Theodosius the Great, had been replaced by leaders of Germanic origin, and control of the peninsula
was in the hands of Odoacer. Theodoric the Ostrogoth however
succeeded in establishing himself not as Emperor, nor as an independent ruler, such as his contemporary Clovis in France, but as
the representative of the Roman Emperor in Constantinople. So
well did he rule that he did indeed deserve to be called a 'righteous
Emperor', said his younger contemporary Procopius writing in the
sixth century.

While Italy and the West were in the hands of these new settlers,
the East was more fortunate. The successful reign of Theodosius II
(408–450) with its care for learning and foundation of the university,
its sound administration, its extension of the city boundaries and
erection of the massive fortified walls on the land side of Constantinople, was in contrast to the less happy fate of the sister capital of
Rome.

But the eastern half of the Empire was not without its difficulties.
It looked at one point in the later fifth century as though the Germanic element, already present in some strength within the Empire
both as settlers and as soldiers, would dominate the imperial government itself, as was already happening at Rome; but again large
numbers were diverted to the West. More important still, the East
could draw on its own native highlands of Asia Minor both for
soldiers and for leaders, who successfully countered the German
Aspar and his followers. Asia Minor now, as later, proved a tower
of strength to the Empire.

The real problems of the East were of another nature. The vigorous
Sassanian Empire lay hard by its eastern reaches. Both powers
coveted the strategic Caucasian area and manœuvred for allies in
these regions. Both sought to maintain a measure of control in the
desert country bordering on the Roman provinces of Syria, Palestine
and Egypt. Perpetual vigilance and frequent conflict marked relations between Persian and Roman on the eastern frontiers, but to
the Romans the Persians were a very different foe from the barbarians who flooded into the Empire. They had a tradition and a
civilisation comparable to that of the Graeco-Roman world. In the
late sixth century the Roman historian Theophylact Simocattes
could write, 'From the very beginning Divine Providence caused the
whole world to be illuminated by two eyes from above, that is, by
the most powerful kingdom of the Romans and by the most wise
sceptres of the Persian polity.'

Even more serious than the ambitions of the militant Persian

Empire was the acute discontent within the eastern provinces. Growing resentment at Roman rule was particularly marked in Syria, Palestine and Egypt and was fundamentally due to local consciousness of an affinity with an oriental and not a western, or Graeco-Roman, way of life. This separatism was shown in various ways, such as the development of national languages and literature, which appear side by side with the international medium, Greek. In Egypt the native language, Coptic, was widely used for everyday purposes and was often the only language understood or read. In large monasteries where there were probably both Greek and Coptic speaking monks and where many visitors from the Mediterranean world might be expected, there would be interpreters. Differences of language, custom and idiom, as well as political antagonisms, were sharply reflected in religious problems from the fourth century onwards. The first General Church Council in 325 had been called by Constantine the Great to discuss and pronounce upon questions of doctrine and organisation. This conciliar method, though not the only way of settling ecclesiastical difficulties, was widely followed throughout the middle ages. The Christian Church, when it received imperial recognition in 313, was already well organised. The lead was taken by the bishops of the great centres of Rome, Antioch and Alexandria, and in the course of the fourth century Constantinople rapidly secured a place for itself in the first rank. In the General Council of Constantinople of 381, and again at Chalcedon in 451, it was recognised that the see of St Peter had primacy of honour, but so rapidly had Constantinople grown in prestige and importance that it now ousted Alexandria and Antioch and took the second place. 'The bishop of Constantinople shall have the primacy of honour after the bishop of Rome, because the same is New Rome' (Council of Constantinople 381, canon 3), which was a bitter blow to the Patriarchs of Alexandria, 'the uncrowned kings of Roman Egypt'.[1]

As Constantine the Great had found, it was by no means easy to inculcate harmony and unity into the Christian Church. Many still followed one or other of the pagan religions, and many were sceptical of any religion at all. The Church had to face the renewed attack of clear-headed and able thinkers, and partly for this reason, partly in response to its own teaching needs, it had to articulate and define its doctrine. The centre of its teaching was the Christian God, and the Church met its greatest difficulties when it attempted to define the nature of God. In stormy meetings of the councils the bishops, most of them from the eastern sees, for in comparison the

1. N. H. Baynes, *Byzantine Studies*, p. 97.

West was as yet less populated and less well organised, hammered out for the guidance of their own and future generations the definitions of the Trinity and particularly of its Second Person, God the Son. The age-long antagonisms of the great ecclesiastical centres, rising political hatred, and even personal rivalries resulted in turbulence and bitter dissension. But Bibles hurled at opponents and the vivid recording of beards plucked out and fractured limbs, must not obscure the constructive work of these churchmen. Their precise formulation of Christian doctrine laid the foundations on which Christian teaching and theology still build today.

The fourth-century discussions about the Trinity were evoked by Arius and his followers who maintained that God the Son was less than God the Father. From the fifth to the seventh century christological controversy raged. In particular there were the two extremes, those who stressed a single nature (monophysites) and those who stressed two separate natures (Nestorians, after Nestorius who figured prominently when this dispute broke out in the early fifth century). Finally, in opposition to both these views, a solution was propounded in 451 at the General Council of Chalcedon which proved acceptable to Rome and Constantinople, though only to a minority in the East Mediterranean. In Syria, Palestine, and Egypt there were a variety of dissident interpretations exaggerated by political discontent which may have been one of the reasons why these regions were eventually lost to the Roman Empire at the time of the Arab attacks. Side by side with the 'orthodox' church, separate churches were set up with their own hierarchy, as the monophysite churches in Egypt and in Syria, some of which exist to this day.

Thus Christianity found that imperial protection, followed by recognition as the one true faith, had brought neither unity nor peace. The close union of Church and State had introduced fresh problems. It had strengthened the position of the Church, had given it new opportunities at home and in the mission field, increased its material resources and secured its pre-eminence. But the inevitably close contact with the things which were Caesar's introduced political issues. The oecumenical councils could now even proclaim the preeminence of this or that see *because* it was 'imperial', 'honoured with the sovereignty and the senate', and not by reason of any Apostolic foundation (though there was no explicit denial of this, and later, in order to hold its own with the older sees, Constantinople tried to maintain that it had a special connection with St Andrew[1]). This close

1. The legend of Constantinople's connection with St Andrew is first found in the seventh century.

association with the State also affected doctrinal issues, as events in
Justinian's reign were to show.

3. THE EMPEROR JUSTINIAN AND THE SIXTH CENTURY

'We have good hope that God will allow us to reconquer the lands
of the old Roman Empire which have been lost through indolence'
(*Novel* 30, 11). Justinian was of Macedonian peasant stock, but like
others before and after him he was fired by the ideal of a Christian
Roman Empire restored to its old boundaries and position of pre-
dominance in the Mediterranean world. For most of his uncle
Justin I's reign (518–527) and then for nearly forty years as sole
ruler, he made the last spirited attempt to re-establish Roman control
over the Germanic peoples now settled in Italy, France, Spain and
North Africa. He had an added incentive in the appeals which came
to him from Catholics who claimed that they were persecuted by
their Arian masters, the Ostrogoths in Italy and the Vandals in
North Africa. To Justinian the support of orthodoxy was no less a
duty than the restoration of imperial authority.

Mustering all his resources in 533 he sent his loyal and able
general Belisarius to launch campaigns which broke Vandal control
of North Africa; here restored Roman rule gave the provinces a
measure of peace and good government which lasted for more than
a hundred years until the Arab conquest. Then after repeated efforts
(535–555), first under Belisarius, then under the more subtle Narses,
the Ostrogoths in Italy were conquered, the islands of the western
Mediterranean were regained, and a foothold was won in south-east
Spain, though most of this country remained in Visigothic hands, as
did the south of France. Indeed the lost province of Gaul was never
to be regained.

Justinian is often criticised for his reconquest and charged with
failure to adapt imperial policy to a changed political situation. He
should, his critics maintain, have concentrated on Greece and the
Balkans and the problems of the eastern frontier and the eastern
provinces. But no Roman Emperor could be expected to relinquish
whole provinces and more without a fight, particularly Italy, for
long the centre and core of the Empire, and, even if not now so
strategically placed as formerly, still the seat of the first capital, Old
Rome. In this Justinian was following in his predecessor's footsteps;
Zeno for instance certainly did not recognise either Odoacer or
Theodoric the Ostrogoth as independent rulers in Italy, but merely
as his governors. After Justinian's day Emperors in the seventh

century still set great store by Italy and the West and considered its reconquest to be within the bounds of practical possibility. It is true that Justinian's régime was hated in Italy and the north fell to the Lombard invaders soon after his death. But it was due to his enterprise that direct political contacts with Italy were renewed. Part of Italy remained in Byzantine hands until the eleventh century, and the cultural links which had long bound South Italy and Sicily to the Aegean world were immeasurably strengthened.

The vigour and scale of the western design should certainly not be taken as indicating freedom from anxiety on other frontiers. The problems of Justinian's reign bear a marked resemblance to those of any Roman Emperor whether of medieval or classical times. Unceasing vigilance was demanded by the enemy in the East, at that time the vigorous Sassanian Emperors of Persia, and in the North by reason of the restless migratory tribes who unceasingly made their way across the Danube into the imperial provinces to pillage and even to settle. Further, the provinces were in a perpetual ferment of political discontent and religious controversy which undermined their loyalty to Roman rule and complicated relations between the various major patriarchates, particularly Rome and Constantinople.

Though his western ambitions were in the foreground, Justinian could not afford to neglect the East. For the greater part of his reign his Sassanian opponent was the able and cultured Chosroes I (531–579). Belisarius' secretary Procopius has left detailed accounts of the intermittent and long-drawn-out Persian wars. By the peace of 562 Justinian did at least retain control over Lazica, the area at the south-east end of the Black Sea with its Christian population and its strategic importance both for politics and for trade. He also maintained the Roman eastern provinces intact in the face of a powerful Persian enemy. But this was only at the cost of expensive military campaigns, supported by unending diplomacy, judicious subsidies and reinforced frontier defences.

In the North, as in the East, Justinian's policy was in the main defensive. He had little time for any effective military drive in this quarter, but was content with a somewhat opportunist policy, designed to check from time to time the Slav and Avar intruders who were continually penetrating deep into the Roman provinces on their plundering raids. The problem of the Slavs and the Balkans was left for his successors.

Justinian was aptly called 'the Emperor who never sleeps'. His ambitious offensive in the West, the continued crises and wars in the North and East might well have fully occupied his programme.

But not so. He himself played a prominent part in the ecclesiastical disputes which arose in the sixth century. Rome had already taken the lead in drawing up the orthodox definition of the relation between the divine and human natures in Christ which was promulgated at the General Council of Chalcedon (451). This definition was not accepted by certain of the eastern Roman provinces, and a good deal of Justinian's time was taken up in trying to find some way of conciliating Syria, Palestine and Egypt without antagonising Rome and the West. He himself was something of a theologian and keenly interested in theology; he was even more interested in finding a *via media* which would save the unity of the Empire.

As far as the monophysite and separatist East was concerned, it had a staunch ally in Justinian's wife Theodora (†548). An ex-ballet dancer with a colourful past, she had travelled in monophysite lands before her marriage, and was partial to the monophysites. She had too a strong streak of political common sense and the courage of her convictions, as she showed on more than one occasion, notably when she was amongst those who persuaded Justinian to stand his ground in Constantinople when the people were rioting in the Hippodrome and threatening to install a rival Emperor. Theodora may have thought it more important to placate the East than to keep on good terms with Rome; it was not until after her death that Justinian took the lead in certain ecclesiastical pronouncements which proved a failure, since they antagonised Antioch, Alexandria and Rome. Justinian however went his way and exercised firm control over the Church; he is one of the few Roman Emperors to whose religious policy the much abused word 'caesaropapism' may fairly be applied.

Well served by able, and sometimes learned, subjects Justinian managed to raise the money for his foreign policy and for the placation of his ring of enemies. He carried out a widespread building programme, ranging from new fortifications in the Peloponnese and a reliable water supply in Ephesus to the erection of Hagia Sophia, the cathedral dedicated to the Holy Wisdom, which is still one of the glories of Constantinople. Many of his laws show his concern to weed out administrative corruption. The legal commission which he set up produced a set of books known as the *Corpus* of Justinian. This was an attempt to straighten out and bring up to date the highly complicated, and by then often contradictory, Roman legal system. The *Corpus* consisted of the *Codex*, a collection of the imperial edicts from Hadrian onwards, including those of Justinian to date, the *Digest* which tried to classify the rulings of the Roman jurists, the *Institutes,* a handbook for the use of law students, and the *Novels* (the *novellae leges*), the edicts of Justinian which had been issued since the publication of the *Codex,* the first volume of the *Corpus* to appear. This *Corpus Juris Civilis* provided the foundations on which later Byzantine codes were built; parts at least of it were used in those Slav countries which came within the Byzantine sphere of influence; and from its reception in the West in the twelfth century it exercised a formative influence on the legal and political thought of Latin Christendom.

In one sense Justinian was the last Roman Emperor. He had succeeded in recovering for the last time an *imperium romanum* embracing almost all the Mediterranean world. The magnificence of his policy and the achievements of his subjects, whether generals and administrators, architects and mosaic artists, poets or jurists, left a great impression on their own and later generations. Dante writing at the end of the thirteenth century thought of Justinian as the representative of the Roman Empire and as such he takes his place in the *Paradiso.*

But Justinian's work for all its splendour marks the close of the late Roman, or early Byzantine, period. Justinian's immediate successors had to grapple with the problems of drastic reorganisation in order that the Roman Empire might adapt itself to the changes introduced by the barbarian kingdoms in the West and strengthen itself to meet fresh challenges from the North and from the East. Any return to the old territorial boundaries was out of the question. Nevertheless the Empire's recuperative powers, its economic resources, its vitality and creative strength, made it possible to adapt its political framework so that the imperial tradition and the cultural life of the Aegean world experienced no violent break in the eastern half of the Empire and passed unawares from late antiquity to early medieval Christendom.

4. THE STRUGGLE FOR EXISTENCE IN THE SEVENTH CENTURY: THE PROBLEMS OF THE HOUSE OF HERACLIUS

Justinian's immediate successors in the sixth and seventh centuries were able realists who reshaped the Roman Empire and ensured its continuity. They did not live on in the popular imagination as Justinian did, and scant justice has been done to the courage and imagination with which they faced a difficult situation. They had to deal with a financial deficit at home and renewed attacks on several fronts. The Lombards invaded Italy in 568 and set up their principalities in the north and centre, though the Empire succeeded in saving the vital strip of territory running from Ravenna to Rome, as well as the lands in the more hellenised south. By the early seventh century the territory recently regained in Spain was again in Visigothic hands and permanently lost. The infiltration of the Slavs into the Balkans continued apace.

Losses in the West made it all the more important to safeguard the eastern borders and here the Byzantines more than held their own. They refused to continue payment of the tribute which Justinian had promised, and after a long-drawn-out war they were able to make a favourable treaty by which they acquired part of Persian Armenia (591), thus strengthening their position in territory which was a fruitful source of military recruits. This was all the more welcome since it was essential to find supplies to take the place of German soldiers who had by now moved elsewhere.

If the Emperor Maurice had built Hagia Sophia, had been portrayed in the living mosaics of San Vitale in Ravenna, and had commissioned the *Corpus Juris Civilis* perhaps we should speak of 'the age of Maurice' and not 'of Justinian'. His reign was only half the length of Justinian's, yet it was sufficient to display qualities of statesmanship which consolidated the essential core of the Empire. It was Maurice who seized his opportunity in Persian politics and supported the young ruler Chosroes II, bringing the long war to a successful end. In Italy and in North Africa his reorganisation did much to safeguard what was left by the creation of the exarchates of Ravenna and of Carthage. The authority of the Exarch, the governor of these provinces, was strengthened by giving him entire control of both civil and military affairs, a system which was extensively employed in the following century in order to facilitate the urgent defence of Asia Minor against the threat of conquest first by the Persians, and then by the Arabs.

Maurice faced the problem on the northern frontier. Here Roman subjects south of the Danube were daily threatened by bands of plundering Avars and Slavs. The Avar kingdom was by now established north of the Danube and the Slavs, whether independent, or under Avar suzerainty, on the middle or lower Danube. By the end of the sixth century the Slavs, like the Germans before them, were settling within the Empire. Maurice's campaigns to drive the Slavs back were cut short by his deposition and subsequent execution after a revolt by his mutinous troops, who could not sustain the discipline and hardships imposed by prolonged campaigns on the northern frontier.

He did not spend time or money on launching grand-scale schemes for the reconquest of the West; but he was by no means indifferent to the age-long Roman claims to universal rule. The will which he drew up in 597 showed that he evidently hoped to use Rome as well as Constantinople as a capital from which imperial authority was to be exercised through a resident Emperor. His second son was to live in Rome, his eldest son remaining in the more important eastern capital. This was not to be. Maurice's death was followed by a time of anarchy (602–610) during which city factions, political disorder and religious disputes created such internal chaos that it looked as though the eastern half of the Empire would fall to the Slavs and Avars from the North and the Persians from the East. Chosroes II, furious at the execution of his friend and ally Maurice together with his whole family, ravaged Syria and Palestine, as well as Asia Minor.

This total disruption was prevented by the arrival of Heraclius, the son of the Exarch of North Africa. Heraclius and the late tenth-century Basil II have been considered the greatest of Byzantine rulers; but whereas Basil II found himself in the full flood of Byzantine success, Heraclius was faced with a situation so grave that at one point it even looked as though he would have to transfer his capital residence from Constantinople to Carthage. He saved the Empire by his able use of his resources. He allied with the Church and exploited to the full Christian crusading zeal against an infidel enemy who had captured Jerusalem and carried off the Holy Cross. In the course of the seventh century the provinces of Asia Minor (such as were not in enemy hands) were grouped together into large military zones under the supreme command of a military governor (the *strategos*), and these were called themes (after the name of a military unit, the *thema*). Expediency later made it necessary to subdivide these great zones in Asia Minor to prevent too much power being concentrated in the hands of one man. The system of themes was, however, gradually extended to the whole Empire during the course of the seventh and later centuries. There is no formal record of such reorganisation, and often the first mention of a new theme is found in some chronicle or saint's life. At the same time soldiers appear to have been established on small farms which they held on condition of military service, passing on land and obligation to their eldest son and thus providing a native army.

What was in essence the militarisation of the Empire formed the basis of its organisation during the middle Byzantine period and also the means whereby it evolved an efficient fighting and naval force. Further, soldier-farmers had an economic and social as well as a military significance. They increased the body of small-holders working the land and contributed to the strength of a free peasantry who must have formed the backbone of the village community provided for by the *Farmer's Law* which very probably belongs to the late seventh century.[1] This was a taxable unit and the central government was perpetually struggling to ensure its continued prosperity and to prevent the lands of free small-holders from being eaten up by the powerful magnates of Asia Minor and elsewhere.

This building up of a native fighting force and the reorganisation of provincial government and boundaries was necessarily a lengthy process and spread over a period of two hundred years or more. Heraclius and his son and grandson must often have failed to see any end in sight, but it was on their foundations that the outstanding achievements of the tenth century stood.

Heraclius, after campaigning in Asia Minor and Mesopotamia over a period of years, successfully crushed Persian ambitions, and in 629 he triumphantly entered Jerusalem with the Holy Cross which the infidels had borne off when they took this city in 614. But Persian defeat did not secure any measure of security, for a more vigorous and dangerous enemy appeared with the rise of Islam. Mohammed died in 632. Neither Persia nor Byzantium could stem the powerful drive of his followers who rapidly established themselves in Persia, Syria, Palestine, and Egypt. Raids into Asia Minor and assaults on the Aegean islands culminated in a bid for the capital. From 674 to 678 Constantinople was blockaded, but the Byzantine fleet defeated the Muslims in 678, a victory as significant for European civilisation as the similar stand in 718 at Constantinople or the check inflicted at Poitiers in 732.

Even so, Byzantium had permanently lost certain of its provinces. The Roman Empire was reduced to only a fragment of the *pars orientalis*, for by the end of the seventh century the Muslims had Syria, Palestine, Egypt and North Africa and everything in the West had gone, except parts of Italy (the Exarchate of Ravenna, a narrow strip joining this to the Duchy of Rome, and lands in the south with Sicily). This was not without its compensations. With the seats of the eastern patriarchates, Antioch, Jerusalem and Alexandria, in Muslim hands, Constantinople became increasingly important as the ecclesiastical centre of the Eastern Churches and determined policy in a way that would not have gone unchallenged in the great days of fifth-century Alexandria. The loss of the eastern provinces with their

1. This is much disputed, but there is general agreement that the *Farmer's Law* belongs either to the late seventh or the early eighth century.

obstinate separatism and their perpetual heresies made it easier to find a doctrinal *modus vivendi* with Rome. And it was now possible to concentrate on more essential problems nearer home, such as the defence of Asia Minor, the indispensable reservoir of men and wealth, or the establishment of some kind of control over the Slav peoples in the Balkans and to the North. It is possible that the loss of the eastern provinces was the salvation of the East Roman Empire.

During the seventh century the Slavs were beginning to settle immediately south of the Danube. There is also evidence—though not all are agreed about this—that from the seventh century onwards the Slavs flooded south into the Peloponnese, either swamping the Greek natives or driving them into temporary exile, to the islands and perhaps to South Italy and Sicily; but however this may be, Greece never became dominated by Slavs to the extent of losing its Hellenic traditions and language. The later Heraclians, particularly Constans II (641–668) and Justinian II (688–695, 705–711), managed to establish partial control in the Balkans, and they made use of this influx of man-power. Slavs were recruited into the army and they were also settled as military small-holders in Asia Minor. But though in this respect the Empire could turn the invasions to its advantage, only some of the newcomers were assimilated into the Empire as subjects; many others remained in virtual independence in the young Slav principalities being formed in the once imperial lands south of the Danube. Further, towards the end of the seventh century the arrival of new and aggressive settlers, the Bulgars, of Turkic stock, brought an added threat to Roman security which reached its climax in the challenge of the First Bulgarian Empire of the early tenth century.

With one short interval, the house of Heraclius had ruled for a hundred years (610–711). Its four great Emperors were self-willed and autocratic, with a morbid streak in their make-up, but each had made his distinctive contribution to the shaping of the medieval Roman Empire. Heraclius' invigorating military and administrative reorganisation saved Constantinople from the Persians; Constans II bore the brunt of the first Arab attacks and still found time to check the Slavs in the Balkans; Constantine IV saved the capital from Arab conquest and restored the prestige of the East Roman Christians; Justinian II stemmed both Arabs and Slavs and continued the policy of infusing fresh blood into the Empire by wholesale transplantation. Thanks to this forceful and statesmanlike dynasty the Arabs were kept out of Europe. The political and cultural continuity of what was predominantly a Graeco-Roman tradition survived unbroken the assaults of invaders on the land frontiers of North and East, reinforced by constant attack by sea. Constantinople was often a 'beleaguered' city; but it did not fall until 1204, and then to a Christian enemy.

II

THE MEDIEVAL ROMAN EMPIRE
717–1056

I. THE ACHIEVEMENTS OF THE ICONOCLAST EMPERORS
717–842

The last Heraclian ruler, Justinian II, lost his throne and life because of his excessive cruelty and increasing tyranny, and with him the dynasty fell. Internal confusion and competition for the throne proceeded apace side by side with renewed Arab attacks. In 717 the able and powerful general of the Anatolikon troops in Asia Minor, who came of a family originally from North Syria,[1] was crowned Emperor as Leo III. He had scarcely made himself master of the capital when it was again besieged by the Muslims.

The famous defence of Constantinople in 717 against the Arabs was only part of the hundred years' struggle from the mid-seventh century to the mid-eighth century, and in this sense the achievement of the later Heraclians and the eighth-century Isaurians is one. The work of the robust and vigorous 'saracen-minded' Leo III (717–741) and his more subtle son Constantine V (741–775) consolidated Roman rule in Asia Minor, taking full advantage of upheavals in the Muslim world whereby the Caliphate was transferred from the Umayyads of Damascus to the Abbasids in Baghdad. Leo III's past experience had made him well aware of the urgency of securing Asia Minor from Arab attack and in the usual Byzantine tradition he employed both diplomacy and military resources. He knew the value of enlisting the goodwill of his neighbours, and his son, Constantine V, actually married the daughter of the Khan of the Khazar

1. A late source says that he came from Isauria in south-east Asia Minor, hence the name 'Isaurian' by which this dynasty is often known.

kingdom dominating the northern Caspian area. After Constantine's death, Byzantine advantages in the Armenian and Mesopotamian regions were not pressed home and from now on to the mid-ninth century there were constant ups and downs, with serious losses such as Crete (c. 827), but Asia Minor stood firm and the Byzantino-Muslim frontier was to some extent stabilised. For more than a hundred years it stretched west of the Caucasian principalities between the Black Sea and the Caspian, running south to the western shores of Cilicia, but not including control of the Taurus Mountains. Here guerilla warfare and border raids organised by marcher lords went on side by side with the economic and social activities of a frontier area, and were later immortalised in the Byzantine epic of the warrior Digenis Akritas. Constantinople had, as it were, come to terms with the East in the sense that it had at least saved Asia Minor, thus making possible the successful offensive in the great days of the tenth-century Macedonians.

With the Slavs of the North the problem was different. The Muslims were not open to conversion, but the migratory pagan Slav peoples owed no binding allegiance to a Christian God or a Mohammedan Allah and their ways of life were at first those of semi-nomads. They offered important fields for missionary enter-prise as well as for the extension of political and cultural influence, and as they moved south and crossed the Danube in great numbers, first as devastating raiders, then as settlers, they became a vital factor in the internal development of the Byzantine Empire. Before the eighth century they were already settling in those Balkan lands which were to become their permanent home. The earliest state to threaten Constantinople was Bulgaria, formed of a fusion of Slav and Bulgar. In the eighth and early ninth centuries this was not yet sufficiently established to constitute a serious political threat. Both Slavs and Bulgars did however demand constant military vigilance and Constantine V was particularly revered, heretic though he was, as a successful general in a series of Balkan campaigns which put some check to Bulgarian raiding activities.

The Isaurians were administrators as well as soldiers. They de-veloped further the reorganisation of the provinces which appears in the seventh century. The new themes in Asia Minor, as these re-grouped provinces were called, were dangerously large and these were subdivided, and the system was gradually extended to other parts of the Empire. Their legal handbook, the *Ecloga*, was an attempt to provide a practical manual for everyday use; it was based on Justinianian law but also reflected certain subsequent changes, as for instance in the penalties inflicted. It was subsequently incorporated in part into later collections and handbooks, though it remained unacknowledged because it was the product of a heretic Emperor. The *Ecloga* was also used in translation by neighbouring Slavonic peoples.

Forced to perpetual vigilance in the eighth century, Byzantium yet had great wealth and economic resources: her geographical position favoured a vigorous and lucrative trade as did her production of much sought after luxury commodities, such as her finely wrought ivories or subtly designed materials, brocades and silks. Her naval strength at first enabled her to direct Mediterranean trade into the channels she favoured, and a deliberate policy of discrimination against Egypt and Syria was adopted. Trebizond and the Black Sea became the important outlets for the far eastern trade, Cherson in the Crimea for Russia and the route to the North. In the West the carrying trade was no longer mainly in the hands of 'Syrians', Greek or Egyptian merchants and others from the East Mediterranean, but was distributed by Italian maritime cities, such as Venice, or those in Byzantine South Italy, as Amalfi or Naples.

The Isaurians were slandered by succeeding generations of Byzantines and their constructive achievements forgotten or ignored because they pursued a religious policy which was doctrinally at variance with orthodox Christian teaching. This inaugurated a period of bitter strife within the Empire and poisoned relations with Rome and the West. In some ways the problem as to whether icons, or pictures of the saints and Christ, could properly be used in Christian worship, was not new. Such use was obviously open to abuse, in that the ignorant might identify the icon with its prototype, or give to it that worship which was owed to God alone. This had been pointed out in a seventh-century council, and by individuals, but it had however been recognised that the right use of such icons was legitimate. The seventh-century Leontius, bishop of Neapolis in Cyprus, when he was refuting the Jews who were accusing the Christians of idolatry wrote, 'We do not say to the Cross or the icons of the saints "You are my God." For they are not our gods, but opened books to remind us of God and to His honour set in the churches and adored.'[1] Moreover, as eighth-century supporters of the icons were to show, denial of their use would lead to theological difficulties, for if the Word really became flesh and dwelt among us, if Christ became man, then He could be represented.

The attempt first to limit, and then to suppress, the use of icons in the eighth century may have been partly due to Muslim and possibly

1. Quoted by N. H. Baynes, *Byzantine Studies*, p. 232.

to Jewish influence. It was certainly strongest in the Asia Minor lands and it was by no means something merely imposed from above by imperial command. Constantine V in the mid-eighth century, rather than his father Leo, was the real protagonist of the iconoclasts and he was supported by a large section of the episcopate, as well as by many of his soldiers and on the whole the non-European population. He very cleverly organised his party, encouraging debates at the end of which his opponents were taken into protective custody, himself writing theological tracts, and trying to win over the obstinate monastic leaders—for he did not want martyrs. He held a church council in 754 attended by 338 bishops and here it was stressed that the iconoclast policy was in full accord with the orthodox tradition. The Pope and the West, particularly Italy, held aloof. It suited the Carolingian rulers to take great offence, and Charles the Great later posed as the champion of orthodoxy in the West, even after the heretical doctrine had been fully renounced at the seventh Oecumenical Council at Nicaea in 787. The movement broke out again in the ninth century but in a milder and more spasmodic form, and once again, this time finally, orthodoxy was restored at a church Council in 843.

The great champion of the traditional use of icons was the church father, St John of Damascus, and in a series of famous treatises he formulated the theological arguments for the use of icons, providing an armoury on which later iconodules freely drew in their defence. St John lived in Muslim territory, though he spent the last part of his life in a monastery near Jerusalem, and he was therefore beyond the range of imperial attack. The monastic leader within the Empire was St Theodore of the Studite house in Constantinople and he suffered exile several times by reason of his outspoken and unshakeable devotion to icons. There was however another implication which both John of Damascus and Theodore the Studite were quick to seize upon—namely the right of the Church alone to decide matters of doctrine. Finally the controversy ended in a compromise—the traditional interdependence of Church and State emerged unchanged, and the age-long use of icons was restored, though with due emphasis on the distinction between the worship which belongs to God alone and the veneration which may be given to the creature or created object.

Byzantium had returned to orthodoxy, but the effects of the controversy were long felt, particularly abroad. In 732 the Byzantine Emperor Leo III had transferred the dioceses of South Italy and Illryicum from papal jurisdiction to that of the Patriarch of Constantinople. This was for long a bitter grievance of the Papacy and complicated relations between Rome and Constantinople in the following century. Further, the fact that the Roman Emperors were heretics (as well as their preoccupation on other fronts) had led the Papacy to seek help, unwillingly, perhaps, from the Frankish rulers of the West. Thus the Carolingians were brought into Italian politics and into close relations with the Papacy. This emphasised the theoretical nature of the Byzantine claims to a universal Christian Empire, and it was from such beginnings that the rival western 'Empire' was to grow.

But though in the early ninth century Charles the Great could wrest temporary recognition of his imperial title from a hard-pressed Byzantine Emperor, and though the religious upheavals of the ortho-dox world had repercussions on the life of Constantinople until well into the tenth century (despite the settlement of 843), it was the falsely named 'Empire' of Charles that disappeared, while from the mid-ninth century the true Roman Empire steadily advanced from strength to strength to produce what is considered with some justification to be the climax of its medieval achievement. Thus Byzantium had successfully emerged from its seventh- and eighth-century crisis a solid Graeco-Roman world, limited in extent, but strengthened and maintaining its strategic position with one foot in Asia and one in Europe.

2. THE HIGH-WATER MARK OF THE BYZANTINE EMPIRE

(i) *The Amorian and Macedonian rulers*

The years 820–1056 were spanned by two dynasties, the short-lived house of the Amorians and the Macedonian family who ruled for almost two hundred years. In many ways they share the same prob-lems and activities; it is a mistake to distinguish too rigidly between them. Michael III the Amorian (sometimes unfairly called 'the drunkard') was murdered in 867 by Basil, the young groom of peasant origin whom he had befriended and made co-Emperor. This Basil 'the Macedonian' (originally of Armenian stock) was the founder of a dynasty which took such firm root in Byzantine soil that the last of the race, the two elderly sisters Zoe and Theodora, were staunchly supported in spite of their obvious inability to meet the needs of State. The Macedonian house certainly produced variety: Basil I constituted himself in a remarkable way the heir to the Byzantine imperial tradition; his son Leo VI the Wise proved to be a scholar and writer rather than a soldier, and he was interested in following up the legal activities of his father's reign. Constan-

tine VII, the longed-for child of Leo's fourth (and therefore un-
canonical) marriage, was renowned for his care for art and letters,
and above all for the manuals of statecraft in which he sought to
hand on to succeeding generations the principles of Byzantine
diplomacy for use in dealing with its neighbours and enemies and
the age-long court ceremonial appropriate to the various seasons of
the Christian year. Constantine's son Romanus II was short-lived
and perhaps not so irresponsible as would appear; his evil genius
was his wife Theophano, the ambitious and egotistical daughter of
an inn-keeper. Romanus died in 963 leaving two small boys Basil II
and Constantine VIII as his heirs. Eventually the elder, Basil II,
proved himself capable of taking the initiative and was the senior
ruler and dominating factor; his brother Constantine, who like Basil
had been crowned as a small child, had the position of co-Emperor.
It was Basil II who was the last Macedonian ruler of distinction, and
indeed he ranks amongst those to whom the Byzantine Empire was
most indebted.   Soured in early youth by the conspiracies
which he had to face, he never married and grew into a hard and
austere ruler, a first-rate general in relentless pursuit of his military
objectives, a statesman in his dealings with the conquered Bulgarians
or his control of the dangerously powerful families, but without any
of the usual Byzantine interest in intellectual and artistic activities
and despising the customary ceremony of court life. He may have
had his more human side, as the historian Michael Psellus who
moved in court circles suggests, but the predominating impression
is that of a grim and cynical statesman. After Basil II, his brother
Constantine VIII, the co-Emperor, was forced to emerge from his
pleasant life in the background, and he ruled alone (1025–1028). He
had no sons, and his three daughters were the last of their line.
Eudoxia went into a convent and stayed there; Theodora pursued a
like vocation, but was forced out of her nunnery to occupy the
throne in the mid-eleventh century; Zoe, the most notorious and
best known, can be reconstructed to the life from the detailed description given by Psellus, who knew her well, and whose words are
borne out by her striking mosaic portrait now uncovered on the walls
of Hagia Sophia. Zoe, with her smooth unwrinkled skin, her careful make-up, her dimpled chin and amiable expression, was vain,
superstitious, extravagant, lacking in good judgment, and her choice
of husbands or adopted son was dictated by purely personal con-
siderations; Theodora was a nonentity. And so Basil I's line petered
out with these two elderly women, suffered to retain their throne out
of misplaced loyalty to their dynasty.

A Basil I and a Basil II alone could not have sustained between them the singular achievements which added so much to Byzantine prestige in this lengthy period and which would have been impossible without some measure of continuity in the direction of policy. In the tenth century the difficulties created by minorities or the incapacity of adult members of the Macedonian house were solved by the Byzantine system whereby it was possible to have co-Emperors without imperilling unity of government. Usually an imperial child would be crowned, even in infancy; sometimes a general or admiral would become powerful enough to obtain coronation and would assume the position of senior Emperor. During the minority of Constantine VII and afterwards, the Admiral Romanus Lecapenus reigned as Romanus I (919–944) and his tenacity and good judgment saved the situation both at home and abroad, although Constantine VII, who married Romanus' strong-willed daughter Helena, actually went so far as to describe his father-in-law (whom he evidently disliked) as 'a common illiterate fellow'. Later in the tenth century Nicephorus Phocas, one of the most successful commanders on the eastern front and a member of an important landed family, married the regent and queen-mother Theophano, was crowned Emperor and constituted himself guardian of the two little Macedonian Emperors Basil and Constantine. This was entirely in accordance with the working practice of the Byzantine government and the indignant ambassador from Italy in 968, Bishop Liutprand of Cremona, gives a somewhat false impression when he persistently regards Nicephorus II as an upstart who has ousted his two 'masters'. When he was dramatically murdered one snowy night, partly at the instigation of Theophano who may have found his tastes too austere for her liking, his rival John Tzimisces took control of the government and similarly regularised his position by persuading the Patriarch to crown him. John Tzimisces was the last of the effective co-Emperors. Basil II obviously neither needed nor intended to allow any such arrangement; of Zoe's three husbands only one, Michael IV, was really competent to act on her behalf, and unfortunately this time no statesman or general emerged to step into the breach when necessary and to take control of the government.

Imperial authority during the Macedonian period was immeasurably strengthened by this steady dynastic background, helped out by the normal Roman system of associate Emperors, and Byzantium became once again the dominating force in the East Mediterranean. It had already repulsed the Muslim drive into Asia Minor, and the iconoclast heresy which had such obvious affinities with the Semitic

B

viewpoint had been repudiated and to some extent rooted out.
Byzantium was once more accepted as a member of Christendom
and the triumph of the icons was the triumph of Graeco-Roman
spirituality, though not of course to the total exclusion of the cross-
fertilisation of eastern and western influences. It is true that the
Byzantine position in the first half of the ninth century was still
precarious: its influence in Italy and in papal circles was much
diminished; it was suffering severe naval reverses in the Mediterranean at the hands of certain Muslim principalities; and the Slavs
and Bulgars settling in the Balkans could scarcely be said to be
under control. But though Muslim fleets from North Africa were
strong enough to attack such strategic centres as Crete (lost *c*. 827)
or Sicily, and raided South Italy and other Byzantine lands, the
economic strength of Constantinople and its trade with the East, by
way of Trebizond and Mesopotamia, continued to flourish, its links
with Russia were developing and despite the growing strength of
certain Italian maritime cities and some inevitable smuggling, it
continued to regulate their distribution of its highly prized exports.
It had economic resources. It also had administrative continuity, a
highly developed civil service and a system of provincial government
adapted from the seventh century onwards to meet fresh needs, and
above all it had unity of purpose centring in the imperial office with
its accepted responsibilities. On such foundations the Amorians and
Macedonians built.

Their obvious successes were the expansion of the land frontiers
in Asia Minor with the revival of naval power in the East Mediterranean, and the drawing of the Slav worlds of Russia and the
Balkans into the orbit of Byzantine cultural and political influence,
accompanied by another extension of frontier whereby the kingdom
of Bulgaria was incorporated into the Empire. Both achievements
were of great significance; the one delayed, and perhaps to some
extent delimited, Muslim incursion into Europe; the other was a
formative influence in the development of the southern Slavs.

(ii) *Eastern expansion 842–1025*

In the mid-ninth century the frontier in Asia Minor ran south from
where the Black Sea turns north, east of Trebizond to the northern
branch of the Euphrates and then south-west until it reached the
Mediterranean, leaving the Taurus and anti-Taurus range and most
of Cilicia under Muslim control. The warfare of the next two hundred
years on this front was not an unbroken series of Byzantine victories,
but in contrast to the reverses, and at best uncertainties, under the

Heraclian and iconoclast Emperors it represented a triumph for Byzantine military leadership, diplomacy and colonisation. On the military side, Michael III concentrated on strengthening the frontier fortresses, particularly those controlling strategic passes, and the series of campaigns planned by his generals together with the decisive defeat of the emír of Melitene who had raided the Armeniakon theme, inaugurated the forthcoming inroads into Muslim territory. Basil I took Lulum which controlled the important pass of the Cilician gates in the south and this was the first step to effective measures to prevent the annual Muslim raids from their mountain strongholds. He conquered the hostile Paulician heretics settled round Tephrice and Leo VI went a step further by adding the adjacent territory between the two branches of the Euphrates which was made into the theme of Mesopotamia. Romanus I's brilliant general John Curcuas (like the Emperor also an Armenian) pushed into Mesopotamia and Armenia and in spite of the formidable opposition of the emir of Mosul and Aleppo, Saif-ad-Daula, conquered Melitene, and further east a number of towns in northern Mesopotamia (as Martyropolis and Dara) and in 944 attacked Edessa, forcing it to give up the treasured towel (the Mandilion) on which Christ had wiped His face and on which was left the imprint of His features. Thus the Byzantines had advanced well into the Tigris-Euphrates area and begun to control the mountainous Cilician territory.

The success of the Christian armies continued. This was due to a combination of circumstances. Byzantine authority as always rallied any possible ally and exploited to the full inevitable differences of policy or clash of ambitions among Muslim rulers. It might suit both Baghdad and Fatimid Egypt to see the powerful emir of Mosul and Aleppo checked by mid-tenth-century Christian advances into northern Mesopotamia; it might seem wise to Damascus to acknowledge the overlordship of a John Tzimisces driving vigorously into Palestine in 975. Equally important were the impetus and generalship supplied by the propertied families of Asia Minor, spurred on, not only by desire for political influence and careers which successful military leadership would give them, but by the urge for economic expansion which found in the newly conquered territory a more promising outlet than that offered by investment in the state-controlled manufacturing or trading enterprises. This last motive received additional stimulus from imperial attempts to limit the extent to which magnates could buy up the land of the small-holder. Then the persistence and tenacity of a succession of fine generals seemed to give renewed vigour to the militant crusading spirit always present in Byzantine warfare against the infidel. The Emperor Nicephorus II, himself one of the greatest generals of the house of Phocas from Asia Minor, had even suggested that all killed in the holy war should be regarded as martyrs. The military drive on land went side by side with renewed assault by sea and the recovery of strategic centres such as Crete and Cyprus, for long the strongholds of Muslims and their pirate fleets. The building up and maintenance of effective naval resources were essential to the Empire's defence, if only by reason of its many long indented coast lines and the infinity of islands in its waters.

The map of 1025 (see p. 45) when Basil II died showed considerable advances to the north (including a substantial portion of Caucasian territory) now organised as the themes or provinces of Iberia, Vaspurkan, Theodosiopolis and Taron. What was left of the kingdom of Armenia (Ani) was due to lapse to Byzantium on the death of its ruler. Further south were other new provinces—Mesopotamia, Melitene and the Euphrates Cities; while those of Cilicia and Teluch controlled the mountainous southern approaches, and an ancient patriarchal seat was once more in Christian hands in the North Syrian province of Antiocheia. Jerusalem itself was not yet reclaimed from the infidel, but Christian armies were already strong enough to ravage southwards into Palestine. It might well have seemed ludicrous to the Constantinople of the early eleventh century had it been suggested that there would ever be scope for Latin crusaders in Syria and Palestine. It looked at this point as though the Byzantines might themselves go on to regain the Holy Places.

(iii) *Constantinople and the Slavs*

The struggle in the north was very different in character. Here Byzantium was faced with a more tractable enemy who was ready to admire, and willing to learn from, Christian civilisation. The expansion of the Slav peoples into central and south-east Europe brought both trials and opportunities to Christendom. Perpetual vigilance in the mission field had been a Christian and an imperial obligation from the days of Constantine the Great in the fourth century. Ever since the iconoclast controversy and the development of an alliance between the Papacy and Frankish rulers in the eighth century, the Church of Rome and the Church of Constantinople had continually been aware of differences of interest and clashes of policy. Both tried to win the Slavs for their particular branch of the Christian Church and both had their successes in different parts of

Europe. Constantinople produced in the second half of the ninth century missionaries who were devout and scholarly and statesmanlike, the best possible exponents of the Byzantine way of life. Men like Methodius (†885) and Cyril were capable and wise enough to set on foot the work which was eventually to bring Serbia, Bulgaria and Russia under the influence and jurisdiction of the Patriarchate of Constantinople. They also invented for them an alphabet which formed the basis of their written language. The young Churches organised and growing up in these areas thus became members of Christendom with their church service and their early theological literature in their own language, Church Slavonic, and not Greek, though often they used translations from the Greek or adapted for their own use Greek prototypes (as in the case of their saints' lives or ascetical works). The same indebtedness to Byzantium is seen in such Old Slavonic church music as has survived.

The proximity of the Slavs in the Balkans had its disadvantages throughout the long course of Byzantine history. During the early period while the Slavs were establishing themselves within the boundaries of the Empire south of the Danube, Constantinople had to endure several centuries of fierce ravaging of the countryside extending all over Greece and reaching to the walls of the City itself. Then by the second half of the ninth century the kingdom of Bulgaria was strong enough to threaten Byzantium, and in the tenth century it was from this source that the most serious political menace in the north came (later on in the fourteenth century it was Serbia which dreamed of being the heir of the Christian Caesars). Constantinople had much to offer and the lure of its cosmopolitan civilisation and rich Empire was again and again to prove a dangerous invitation to conquest. At first the time-honoured method of an annual subsidy was employed and then in the early tenth century Bulgarian desire for at least some share in the Empire was staved off, first by promises and then by the adroit policy of the Admiral Romanus Lecapenus who was crowned co-Emperor. When the ambitious Bulgarian king Symeon died in 927 his son Peter was married to one of Romanus' grand-daughters, Maria Lecapena (not of genuine 'born-in-the-purple' stock). But Bulgaria was always a thorn in the flesh and to late tenth-century Emperors moving from strength to strength elsewhere it may well have seemed that the safest solution lay in conquest. Between them John I Tzimisces and Basil II reduced their turbulent neighbour and until the revival of national independence nearly a hundred and fifty years later it was part of the Empire and was divided into the provinces of Paristrion and

Bulgaria. Basil II was noted for his cruel and relentless campaigns, but the 'Slayer of the Bulgarians', as he was called, made a statesmanlike settlement in the conquered lands, allowing for local custom and permitting certain conciliatory ecclesiastical arrangements whereby the Church retained much of its virtual autonomy. This brought Bulgaria under immediate control; it also brought the Bogomil heretics rampant there within the immediate jurisdiction of the orthodox Emperor whose bounden duty it was to exterminate all such sources of infection; and it meant too that there was no longer any buffer state between Byzantium and the dangers lurking beyond the Danube.

Constantinople's relations with the Slavs were not confined to Bulgaria. The effect of its missionaries was felt throughout the Balkans, though Croatia and Serbia never became part of the medieval Empire as Bulgaria did. Croatia tended to be drawn northwards into the orbit of Hungary. But the Latin Dalmatian coast (a recognised part of the Empire, though enjoying considerable independence) and the very different Slavonic hinterland both acknowledged Constantinople's claims to political overlordship, the warmth of the acknowledgment varying with the imminence of some such danger as Arab raids from the Adriatic or the threat of Bulgaria's alarmingly rapid territorial expansion.

On the northern shores of the Black Sea Byzantium had long had interests and exercised some control through the strategically placed theme of Cherson in the Crimea. It was for economic and political as well as religious reasons that diplomatic relations were maintained with this area, and from the earliest times of the Christian Roman Empire missionaries and then ecclesiastics had been sent to the peoples here, whether migratory or settled—Khazars, Ugro-Finnish and others. The Hungarians when they finally found their home within the encircling Carpathians had already in the course of their wanderings come into contact with orthodox Christianity. Trade with the northern lands whose waterways linked the Black Sea and the Baltic flourished by way of Kiev and Novgorod and special trade treaties exist which were made in the tenth century; men from the north served as mercenaries and also in the late tenth century constituted the Emperor's renowned Varangian bodyguard; and as the principality of Kiev took political shape diplomatic contacts were established. Here in Russia Constantinople never exercised direct control, but she was responsible for introducing orthodox Christianity and bringing the young Kievan church under the jurisdiction of the Patriarch of Constantinople. The rulers of Kiev were deliberately cultivated and the tenth-century diplomatic handbook of instructions for the Byzantine foreign office shows that great importance was attached to good relations in this quarter. When the newly converted Princess Olga visited Constantinople in 957 she was given a magnificent reception. In 989 the timely help of the Russian contingent in the war against Bulgaria was rewarded by what was in those days the unheard of prize of a Byzantine imperial princess to wife; Vladimir of Kiev married Anna the sister of Basil II and pledged both himself and his people to the adoption of Christianity.

(iv) *Byzantium and the West*

Byzantine expansion in the East and among the Slavs had no parallel in the West. Here in Italy her position seemed at best to be a precarious maintenance of the *status quo* and was often seriously threatened by the tenth-century Saxon rulers of Germany who had inherited the mantle of the Carolingians. Otto I was crowned, first king of the *regnum Italicum* (the North Italian Lombardy kingdom), and then in 962 Emperor. In spite of opportunities for diplomatic by-play among the small central and South Italian principalities (as Salerno-Capua) Otto I failed in his attacks on the Byzantine provinces of Longobardia (Apulia) and Sicily (now consisting only of the South Italian district of Calabria, since the island of Sicily was in Arab hands). He failed too in his attempts at getting Constantinople to acknowledge his imperial title. His prolonged negotiations are described in the racy and biased account of one of his ambassadors, Liutprand of Cremona, and the most he gained was a Byzantine wife for his son Otto II, Theophano, who came from one of the great landed families and not, as he had asked, from the imperial house itself. Otto III, the boy born of this marriage, was hoping to marry a Byzantine princess and, before his early death in 1002, had revealed his conception of an Empire centred in Rome, but it is highly doubtful whether it would ever have been possible to set up in the West any serious counterpart to the *imperium romanum* of Constantinople. By the beginning of the eleventh century it was equally impossible for Constantinople to establish any real stronghold in what had once been the *pars occidentalis*. Basil II set about reorganising Byzantine government in the two South Italian provinces which were now united under a governor with the title of catepan, and he certainly had in mind the re-conquest of Sicily from the Muslims. But the Byzantines were not destined either to regain their rule in Sicily or to retain it on the mainland; their immediate political successors in the South were to be the Normans and after the mid-eleventh century their influence in Italy was mainly cultural and diplomatic. To end on a note of failure would perhaps give a false impression. Byzantine stock stood high in western circles: the very confidence of the Byzantine Emperor reflected in Liutprand's reports of his conversations with Nicephorus II in 968, or the conciliatory tone of Pope Leo IX's letter to the most orthodox Emperor Constantine IX in 1054, indicate the security which Constantinople felt and the respect which it commanded, unwillingly or otherwise, from its neighbours.

(v) *Imperial rule at home: church and learning*

Byzantium's acknowledged military and naval successes for more than a hundred and fifty years under the Amorians and Macedonians and the rapidly extending influence of its Christian civilisation were dependent on vigour and initiative in home circles. One of the most striking features of Byzantine life was its robust quality and the variety of its activities. From the mid-ninth century until at least the death of Basil II (1025) the autocratic imperial authority inaugurated significant legal and administrative reforms. Basil I had extensive plans for the 'purification' of the old law. He published a handbook, the *Procheiron*, and subsequently some time after 879 the *Epanagoge* was drawn up.[1] Leo VI completed his father's work in the *Basilica* which was based on earlier collections, particularly those of Justinian. These law books aimed at making Justinianian legislation more easily available and they were in Greek, the current language of the Empire. The *Basilica* was constantly glossed and it was eventually to become the standard authority. Imperial responsibility was all-embracing, and there are many other publications both of an official and an unofficial nature—laws issued throughout the period, or Leo VI's *Book of the Prefect*, or trade agreements, all of which illustrate the nature of imperial control, ranging from the careful regulation of the guilds of Constantinople or the conditions under which Russian merchants might stay in the City, to the still more complex problem of land-ownership.

Purchase of land was bound up with the growth of powerful families, who until the very last days of the Empire commanded resources which were a perpetual challenge to the authority of the State. The possession of landed wealth was by no means exclusively

1. Some scholars maintain that the *Epanagoge* was never officially published. For different views on this see Ostrogorsky, *History of the Byzantine State*, pp. 213–14. On the legal work of the Macedonians see also H. J. Scheltema in *Cambridge Medieval History* IV, pt. II (new ed. 1967), pp. 65 ff.

a lay prerogative; ecclesiastical authorities accumulated extensive resources of this kind, particularly the great monastic foundations, very often with episcopal connivance. Imperial agrarian policy was not at all consistent. Some Emperors, as Romanus I or Basil II, made a bold attempt to check the acquisition of land from the small-holder or farmer with heritable military obligations, partly because it was politically expedient to limit the power of the aristocracy and partly in order to ensure the supply of native soldiers. Basil II, well aware of the political danger of the great families, also made 'the powerful' responsible for the taxes of 'the poor'. Others, either from policy or from lack of authority, did not discriminate against 'the powerful'. For instance Nicephorus II himself came from a landed family and he relaxed the agrarian laws which operated to the advantage of the small-holder. As a first-rate general he was how-ever keenly alive to military needs and therefore anxious to do something to protect the farmer-soldier. He made special rulings concerning the military holdings of Armenian frontier-soldiers, who were allowed to reclaim their land from 'the powerful' or from a monastery even after as long as thirty years' absence; and he drastically limited new monastic foundations, as well as monastic acquisition of landed property whose inefficient cultivation too often caused the loss of taxes to the state treasury.

No longer rent by heresy the Church flourished. The restoration of the orthodox use of icons did not eradicate different shades of opinion among churchmen, but the two main ecclesiastical develop-ments in this period were the Church's steadily growing authority at home and abroad, particularly in relation to the imperial power and the newly established Slavonic churches, and the occasional tension of its relations with Rome. This last development was especially associated with two particular Patriarchs of Constanti-nople, the ninth-century Photius and the eleventh-century Michael Cerularius. The Church could and did check the Emperor, however strong his position. For instance John Tzimisces had to promise revocation of his predecessor's laws limiting ecclesiastical acqui-sition of property and to give up his proposed marriage with the notorious Queen-Mother Theophano before he could get the Patriarch to perform his coronation. The changing iconography of the imperial art of the period also shows the growing authority of the Church. Legal and literary works reflect a relationship which is one of interdependence. John Tzimisces was reported to have said: 'I recognise two authorities in the world, priesthood and Empire; the Creator of the world entrusted to the first the care of souls and to the second the control of men's bodies. Let neither authority be attacked, that the world may enjoy prosperity.'

Secure and strengthened, Constantinople was involved in conflict with Rome by ecclesiastical, as well as secular, policy. Differences of doctrinal emphasis, as the western addition of the words *filioque* to the creed, or of discipline and custom, were sharply brought out by the dispute over the recognition of the Patriarch Photius on his appointment in 858. Photius died in communion with Rome, but the various points at issue, together with the irritating memory of the dioceses removed from papal jurisdiction in 732, lived on, and were often brought to the surface by some chance combination of circumstances or clash of character. In spite of the notoriety achieved by the overbearing eleventh-century Patriarch, Michael Cerularius, the final rift between the two Churches does not really belong to the year 1054, when the arrogant papal legate Cardinal Humbert threw down the bull of anathema in the cathedral of Hagia Sophia, shaking the dust off his feet as he swept out. The 'official' separation may date from 1054 when the church of Constantinople appears to have ceased to pray for the Pope at its communion service, the outward sign of the rift. Surely this could easily be put right, suggested Alexius I in 1089. But then the western crusaders came, and the events of the twelfth century, culminating in the Latin conquest of Constantinople and of other Byzantine territory, made it almost impossible to bridge the gulf.

In learning and art the richness of the period 842–1025 defies description. It opens with the scholar Photius and his literary circle and includes such linguists and philologists as the early missionaries to the Slavs. Surviving manuscripts show the frequent use and copying of classical and later texts, while manuscript illuminations, the Paris Psalter for instance, or Basil II's *Menologion*, show a wide range of style, including much allegorical and naturalistic work influenced by the late Graeco-Roman period. There was almost constant imperial interest and activity. Bardas Caesar provided public funds for the university in the Magnaura Palace; Leo VI was a theologian and poet; Constantine VII supported a flourishing school of historiography and himself wrote his grandfather Basil's life and saw that diplomatic and imperial usage was recorded for future need in the invaluable books on imperial administration and ceremony. Basil II was notoriously allergic to the pursuits of cultivated society, but it is unlikely that this affected letters and learning. Certainly both scholars and humanists are to be found at work not so long after Basil's death in 1025.

III

FUNDAMENTAL CHANGES
1025–1204

I. THE PARTING OF THE WAYS IN THE ELEVENTH CENTURY

Since its remarkable recovery in the seventh century the Empire
had on the whole stood firm: it may have lost some ground in Italy,
but this was more than compensated for by successes in the Balkans
and especially on the eastern frontier. Then in the course of the
eleventh century a new enemy, the Seljuk Turks, broke into Asia
Minor; Slav principalities and peoples in the Balkans were growing
in vigour and independence; the Normans of South Italy launched
hostile campaigns against the Empire, while an embarrassing
crusading fervour against the infidel was mounting in the West.
This time Byzantium did not succeed in maintaining its frontiers
and 1204 was but the harbinger of 1453.

When Basil the Slayer of the Bulgarians died on Christmas Day
1025 it was not at all evident to the Byzantines that far-reaching
changes were imminent. Michael Psellus, one of the liveliest and
most observant of medieval writers, wrote a history of his eleventh-
century contemporaries. He mentioned difficulties and mistakes,
even imperial follies, but had no inkling that Byzantium's future
was one of political decline and disintegration, in contrast to some
writers of the fourteenth century, when sorrow and mortification
were recognised as their common lot. In 1025 a citizen of Constantinople might well have agreed that the Empire's prestige had
never stood higher. As it was, internal and external factors militated
against the maintenance of its tenth-century prosperity, and indeed
in some respects the seeds of future trouble were already present and

clearly discernible in the tenth century, as in the central government's struggle with the powerful landowners.

From 1025 to 1081 when Alexius Comnenus gained the throne, the quality of the Byzantine rulers fell far short of that of the Heraclians or Isaurians, or such Macedonian Emperors as Basil I or Basil II. So strong had popular sentiment for the Macedonian house become that from 1025 to 1056 the dynasty lingered on, represented by Constantine VIII, an irresponsible and pleasure-loving old man, and his two elderly daughters—Zoe, vain and extravagant, and Theodora, a nun dragged reluctant from her convent to occupy the throne jointly with her sister Zoe, to the latter's annoyance. There was no general or statesman with sufficient vigour and good fortune to take control, either as co-Emperor or in his own right. Michael IV, Zoe's second husband, was a tenacious and courageous soldier, but he suffered from epilepsy; George Maniaces, who looked like overthrowing Zoe's third husband Constantine IX, was killed on his way to the capital; Isaac Comnenus, who showed some of the quality of the later members of his house, antagonised first the Patriarch Michael Cerularius and then the populace and the aristocracy in Constantinople, and had to abdicate. Indeed once the firm hand of the old autocrat Basil II was removed, the nobility became more and more dominating. From 1025 to 1081 they fought amongst themselves as to which of them should take control, the families and officials entrenched in the capital, though also possessing lands and privileges throughout the Empire, or the military families with their strongholds and wealthy estates in the provinces and their better understanding of the needs of imperial defence. But it must be remembered that the great magnates of Asia Minor with their formidable bands of retainers had been ruthlessly penalised and crushed by Basil II and their lands confiscated, and for the greater part of this period affairs were dominated by a series of ministers and rulers who were often either ineffective or unfortunate. The story of their triumph over their more military-minded opponents is brilliantly described in the *Chronographia* of Michael Psellus, who as a minister and counsellor of Emperors had taken a hand in making the history of his own times. This struggle is sometimes described as that of the 'civil' versus the 'military' aristocracy, the 'military' rulers being Isaac I Comnenus and Romanus IV Diogenes, both of whom tried to strengthen the defences of the Empire.

The régime of the so-called 'civil' aristocracy had however some redeeming features. Basil II had never bothered to express himself

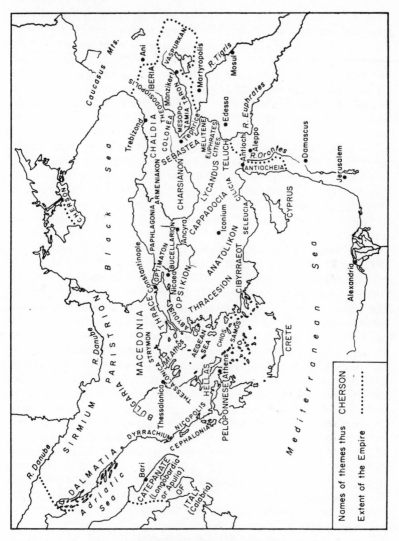

The Byzantine Empire *c.* 1025
(after Ostrogorsky)

elegantly and he affected to despise learning (though he evidently read up anything which interested him, such as military tactics[1]). In reaction to his austerity there was a marked blossoming of intellectual and cultural activities under the open patronage of the later Macedonians and their successors. The court was the centre of this movement and affairs of State were controlled by men of learning, such as Psellus the humanist or John Xiphilinus the jurist. It is therefore not surprising that considerable sums of public money were allocated to the reorganised state-controlled university of Constantinople. Among teachers and scholars, lay and cleric, writers and artists, there was evidently no deterioration but on the contrary steady progress, as is witnessed by memoirs and histories, theological commentaries and polemic, liturgical poetry and music, churches and mosaics, works in ivory and patterned textiles.

There was too a steady growth in the power of the Church. The patriarchate of Constantinople had increased in prestige as its former rivals in the East—Antioch, Alexandria and Jerusalem—declined in power; it had authority over a substantial part of the Slav world whose acceptance of Christianity from the Byzantine missionaries meant submission to the ecclesiastical jurisdiction of the Patriarch of Constantinople. Deep-seated, though not fundamental, differences of custom and rite and theological emphasis between the Churches of Rome and Constantinople were exploited to serve the ambitions of an overbearing Patriarch who had grown too sure of himself. The papal legate sent to Constantinople to deal with this situation was an equally arrogant man, Cardinal Humbert, and an open conflict broke out at precisely the moment when it was most essential for Rome and the Byzantine Empire to pursue a common policy against the Norman invaders of South Italy. Once again Byzantium felt the want of a strong Emperor: Constantine IX failed to control his aggressive Patriarch, and the Roman legates deposited a bull of excommunication in Hagia Sophia. At the time neither side realised the implications of the situation. Indeed the breach was not necessarily final in 1054 and it might have been healed later on had the Normans and the Venetians been less aggressive and less ambitious.

The growing strength of the Byzantine Church was further demonstrated by Michael Cerularius' attempt to subordinate the State to the Church in a way that was contrary to the imperial tradition of East Rome. It was not sufficient for him to assert his

1. Michael Psellus, *Chronographia*, trans. E. R. A. Sewter, pp. 24 ff. (ch. 30, 33, 36).

independence of Rome. He loudly proclaimed that the affairs of the Church were of more importance than those of the State and that they were the concern of the ecclesiastical authorities alone, thus undermining the time-honoured place of the Emperor as guardian and protector of the Church. Cerularius even went further and threatened to depose the Emperor, then Isaac Comnenus; his 'snarlings' were not entirely without success for Isaac shortly after- wards had to abdicate, even though Cerularius himself had mean- while died. The growth of ecclesiastical authority was not in itself anything new; it had been for instance apparent in the days of Leo VI with his marriage problems or John Tzimisces and his promises to the Patriarch before his coronation, but it is more noticeable in the eleventh century because of the unusually spec- tacular aggressiveness of Michael Cerularius which could only have been bridled by a firm imperial hand.

The weakness of the central authority during the years 1025–1081 is evidenced in other ways, and for the greater part of the period was indeed accentuated not only by lack of imperial foresight but by the deliberate policy of those in control in Constantinople. Basil II had been well known for his strict economy and personal austerity; he gave audiences merely in a robe of purple 'with a handful of gems as a mark of distinction' and he had elaborate spiral galleries dug underground to house the overflow of wealth which could not be got into the imperial vaults. His brother Constantine and his niece Zoe and her husband Constantine IX were otherwise; they were notorious for their heedless expenditure, their extravagant vagaries and whims, such as rebuilding the Church of St George the Martyr and then altering the whole plan and rebuilding it yet again on a fantastically magnificent scale. 'Gold flowed from the public treasury like a stream bubbling up from inexhaustible springs.'[1] Psellus frankly admitted that reckless overspending was 'the turning point in the fortunes of the state'. Imperial extravagance would have been sufficient to cause trouble, but at the same time there was also a rise in the cost of administration because the government was constantly creating new posts in the civil service.

While the State's domestic expenditure grew, its income was for various reasons reduced. The underlying reason for this reduction was the failure to keep 'the powerful' under control. Thus various trends, which were clearly discernible even under the far more effective rulers of the earlier Macedonian period, were now given full rein. Basil II had made the well-off and not the village com-

1. Michael Psellus, *Chronographia*, trans. E. R. A. Sewter, p. 189 (ch. 185).

munity responsible for the taxes of their neighbours. This liability was removed by Romanus III who was presumably not strong enough to make 'the powerful' pay up, and the treasury was thus deprived of one source of income. Further reductions in receipts followed the practice of farming out the collection of taxes to a number of private contractors. These took over a good deal of the work which properly belonged to the central government and in consequence both the provinces and the State suffered: the former were squeezed dry; the latter received only a certain proportion of the taxes extorted.

The central authority was further weakened in the eleventh century by the grant of various immunities to private individuals, thus pointing the way to a development which characterises the later Byzantine State. Secular and ecclesiastical estates were granted privileges which exempted them from certain taxes or public obligations. This was not unusual. More important was the granting of land to the care (*pronoia*) of the grantee for a stated period, usually his lifetime. The grantee, or pronoiar, administered it and drew the revenue. The first known instance is in the mid-eleventh century, and by the seventies many such grants were being made in return for a money payment, but there is as yet no mention of any military obligation connected with the grant. Transactions of this kind had not occurred in the great days of the middle Byzantine period, though they are found earlier. They sapped the power of the central authority, and were indeed a sign of its weakness. They should not be confused with gifts of monasteries and their revenues to the laity, originally made by great ecclesiastics to ensure the economic development of monastic property, then by the imperial authority primarily as a means of reward.

Financial needs increased as the century wore on. The deficit due to declining tax receipts and mounting expenditure at court and in administration was met by a shortsighted device—that of debasing the coinage. To do this on a large scale was to undermine Byzantine economy. The prestige and standing of East Rome in international trade was to a great extent due to the reliability of its standard gold coin, the nomisma or bezant. It has long been known that systematic debasement took place from about 1071 onwards and it was usually assumed that this was due to the acceleration of financial difficulties when the Byzantines lost much of Asia Minor to the Seljuk Turks. It has however now been shown by analysing the densities of Byzantine coins that the responsibility for the great debasement really rests with Constantine IX (1042–1055) who reduced the value of the nomisma from 24 to 18 carats.[1] By the time of Psellus' foolish pupil Michael VII (1071–1078) its value had sunk to between 14 and 12 carats.

Landed families and prominent statesmen were afforded various opportunities of enriching themselves. Michael Psellus possessed several grants of monastic property in different parts of the Empire. The failure to enforce any special imperial protection (rather than its deliberate withdrawal) made it more and more difficult for the small-holder with military (or naval) obligations to survive. The small free peasant and the soldier-farmer were increasingly reduced to the status of dependent tenants on a large estate. It was the successful imperial encouragement of the free small-holder which had proved so important a factor in the regeneration of the State from the seventh century onwards and the disappearance of this element hit both the finances and the defences, and introduced changes into the social structure of the Empire. Here again late eleventh-century policy foolishly accelerated this change in an attempt to raise money quickly; those soldier-farmers left were allowed to buy exemption from military service on payment of an agreed sum. The central government did however, both now and long afterwards, attempt to retain its hold over those dependent tenants (*paroikoi*) who had financial obligations to the imperial fisc. It therefore made strenuous efforts to prevent them from settling on ecclesiastical or secular estates where landlords might claim these dues.

For the greater part of the period 1025–1081 the families and ministers in power, whether of the aristocracy or not, had for the most part tried to safeguard their own position by weakening possible opponents. It is true that in an autocratic state such as the East Roman Empire the final responsibility lay with the Emperor, but only if he were a strong and effective ruler. Under the two old Macedonian Empresses and their more immediate successors the antagonism of the ruling party to the military families was all too often reflected in the emphasis of imperial policy. It might for a time have been argued that the frontiers had been expanded and strengthened, not only by the military rulers before 1025, but afterwards. Even Constantine IX had some successes, 'for the boundaries of the Empire were much extended in the East, and a considerable part of Armenia annexed'.[2] Unfortunately the Empire could not afford to neglect its military and naval defences, nor to relax its diplomacy, in view of new enemies on at least three frontiers.

1. P. Grierson, *Byzantinische Zeitschrift*, 47 (1954), pp. 379 ff.
2. Michael Psellus, *Chronographia*, trans. E. R. A. Sewter, p. 190 (ch. 189).

Here, as in other ways, the eleventh century proved a watershed.

On the North the steppe tribes, the Patzinaks, Uzes and Cumans, were pouring over the long Danube frontier and the force of the raids was no longer broken by Bulgaria, now incorporated within the Empire. These nomads were sometimes persuaded to settle as frontier troops but they remained bandits at heart and were a dangerously uncertain quantity, a drain on imperial finances and potential allies for any imperial enemy. The Slavs within the Balkans were another liability: Bulgaria, reduced to provincial status, was discontented; the virtually independent little Slav principalities to the north-west, as Zeta or Croatia, were ready to consolidate their position and to extend their influence by turning to Byzantium's rivals. For instance in 1070 the ruler of Zeta played off Rome against Constantinople by receiving his crown from Pope Gregory VII. Further, though these princelings had for the moment little more than nuisance value, the situation in the Adriatic and beyond was changing in a way which inevitably affected Byzantium. The growing power of Hungary and of Venice meant that Croatia or Zeta or Rašca might be an important factor in Mediterranean diplomacy, and perhaps even challenge the imperial authority itself, as Serbia did in the fourteenth century.

It was in the East that greatest recent advances had been made before 1025. In 1043 the rest of Armenia lapsed to Byzantium on the death of its ruler in accordance with the treaty made with Basil II. Once more a buffer state had become a province. But some twenty years later in 1065 Armenia was annexed by the Seljuk Alp Arslan, thus heralding the systematic raids and conquest of Asia Minor, the backbone of the Empire. In the Middle East the Central Asian invaders, the Seljuk Turks, had subdued Persia and established a military sultanate over the Caliphate. They proceeded to attack the eastern provinces of Byzantium where they at first made more headway than further south against the Fatimids in Egypt. The Seljuks were however divided amongst themselves, and although they defeated the Byzantine Emperor who attempted to drive them out of Asia Minor (at the battle of Manzikert in 1071) they were willing to make a reasonable treaty with him. This might have enabled the Empire to muster its resources, but during his absence on campaign the Cappadocian magnate and Emperor Romanus IV had been deposed by the supporters of the Ducas family at Constantinople who put an obviously unsuitable bookish youth, Michael VII Ducas, on the throne. In these circumstances the Turks repudiated the proposed peace terms and had no difficulty in advancing into Asia Minor.

As though this disaster in the East was not enough, Bari, the last stronghold in the West, fell to the Normans in South Italy in the same year (1071). Here was another enemy as dangerous as the Seljuks, insidious, subtle, ambitious. Having demolished Byzantine possessions on the mainland, the Normans wrested Sicily from the Arabs, and not content with a considerable part of the old Byzantine possessions in Italy, they then turned their eyes to Greece itself. Even Psellus in the midst of his panegyric on the young Emperor Michael VII had to admit that affairs were 'at their lowest ebb', but it is hardly fair to attribute this almost entirely to Michael and his tutor, as another Byzantine historian does.[1] The root of the trouble was the fact that poor statesmanship at home accompanied by the increasing authority of the magnates unfortunately coincided with the appearance of powerful external enemies, notably the Turks in the East and the Normans in South Italy.

2. APPARENT REVIVAL UNDER THE COMNENI

(i) *Alexius Comnenus (1081–1118)*

With the accession of Alexius Comnenus in 1081 the military aristocracy triumphantly came to the fore. Alexius was the ablest of the military magnates, soldier, politician and diplomat, and by his own efforts and by the establishment of a dynasty, he staved off the disintegration of the Empire for more than a hundred years.

The difficulties of government during the sixties and seventies of the eleventh century are apparent in the concluding pages of Psellus' *Chronographia*, however much he tries to gloss over the mistakes of his friends and patrons, the Ducas family. Alexius' immediate problems are equally apparent in the account of his reign written by his daughter, the princess Anna Comnena. The temper of each period is admirably reflected in these two contrasting and masterly works—the *Chronographia* with its eleven Emperors and two tiresome old Empresses in only fifty-six years, and the *Alexiad* dominated by the single central figure of 'my father the Emperor' who ruled with distinction for thirty-seven years before he died in 1118.

Three Comneni, father, son, and grandson, span the years 1081–1180 and their personalities and achievements are deceptive: they blind the onlooker to radical changes in the Byzantine world. The former system of government and defence had gone; feudal and separatist elements steadily grew. The late Byzantine period was the

1. John Scylitzes, *History* (Migne, *Patrologia Graeca*, vol. 122, col. 846); cf. Michael Psellus, *Chronographia*, trans. E. R. A. Sewter, p. 284 (ch. 7).

age of the feudal military aristocracy. It was the military and political leadership of the wealthy landed families which alone was capable of using such resources as were left, and which did for a time enable Byzantium to some extent to hold its own amongst the rising Latin and Slav powers and to check the various Muslim potentates in the Near East.

Anna Comnena does not exaggerate when she makes Alexius say, 'I found the Empire surrounded on all sides by barbarians and absolutely deficient in resources. . . . You all know about the incursions of the Persians (the Turks), the raids of the Scythians (the Patzinaks), and you cannot have forgotten the spears from Longobardia (the old Byzantine province in South Italy) that were whetted against us.'[1] Alexius found not only a depleted treasury, a debased coinage and a government whose authority was seriously undermined, but a ring of enemies, in Italy, in the Balkans and in Asia Minor. In his day at any rate, the most dangerous foes and rivals were to come from the West (the Normans and the maritime Italian cities), but at his accession it was in the East that most damage had already been done. The greater part of Asia Minor was now in the hands of the Turks, thus seriously affecting Byzantine military and naval economic resources; this meant not only a broken eastern frontier but difficulties in military recruitment. The loss of manpower also affected Byzantine maritime strength at a time when it could ill afford to neglect either its naval or its merchant shipping. Its financial troubles were already sufficiently great without further losses due to a decline in trade and customs dues.

Alexius' first concern was with foreign policy: defence, whether by means of diplomacy or arms. He was crowned in April 1081 and his first recorded negotiation was with the Seljuks in Asia Minor, 'the godless Turks' with their headquarters now at Nicaea. At this point all that could be done was to recognise their claims in Asia Minor and to hope to halt further advance in order to have a free hand to deal with the Norman attack. Secure in South Italy, the Norman leader Robert Guiscard had now turned to Byzantium, desiring to become Roman Emperor. 'Normandy indeed begot him, but he was nursed and reared by consummate Wickedness.'[2] The Byzantines would have heartily endorsed Anna Comnena's description of Robert Guiscard and not without reason. Guiscard attacked Greece and Macedonia with some success in spite of the combined activities of Venice and Alexius. His unexpected death in 1085 brought a respite,

1. Anna Comnena, *Alexiad*, VI, 3 (trans. E. A. S. Dawes, pp. 141–2).
2. Anna Comnena, *op. cit.*, p. 26 (I, 10).

but nothing more, in the duel between Constantinople and the Normans. The episode brought out clearly certain factors of some importance in future Byzantine diplomacy: the various small powers in the Balkans were ready to support the highest bidder and had to be watched carefully. And Byzantine maritime deficiencies had to be made good with the help of neighbouring naval powers such as Venice, but this was not cheap. Alexius had to grant the Venetians extensive trading privileges throughout the Empire so that they were on a more advantageous footing than the ordinary Byzantine trader; this was the seed of future difficulties and fomented Byzantine envy of the Latin intruders, while Venice's Italian rivals were promptly stimulated to obtain similar rights in return for their support.

Guiscard's death in 1085, the crushing defeat of a serious Patzinak attack in 1091, and the partition of the Turkish principality of Rum in Asia Minor following the death of its ruler Suleiman, seemed to clear the field for Alexius and to make possible the recovery of some at any rate of the lost territory. But the situation, both for Byzantine and Turks, was radically changed by a bombshell from the West in the shape of the First Crusade.

The reason why there was mutual hostility between Greek and Latin crusaders is to be found in their quite different aims. The crusading movement in the West was encouraged by the highest ecclesiastical authority; it had been preached by Pope Urban II at the Council of Clermont in 1095. Though the Holy Land had for centuries been in infidel hands, pilgrims had normally had access to the Holy Places. Now rising religious zeal in the Latin world wished to drive out the Muslim, and there was the added attraction of territorial gain and an outlet for maritime and colonial enterprise. The reformed Papacy naturally longed for the liberation of Jerusalem, but it may also have had in mind the extension of its own ecclesiastical authority in the East and the healing of the official rift between the two Churches of Rome and Constantinople.

Alexius himself would not have been averse to healing the schism, and in one of his letters to Urban II he does in fact remark that it was strange that the Pope's name had slipped out of the list of those prayed for at mass but it could no doubt be re-inserted. He would however have been reluctant to subscribe to the extension of papal power in the territories belonging to the other patriarchates. Further, he had certainly asked from time to time for mercenaries or auxiliary troops from the West, but not in order to go straight to Jerusalem; he had more pressing calls nearer home. Both imperial tradition and immediate needs made it impossible for a Byzantine Emperor to conceive of a crusade in the western sense. The East Roman outlook differed in at least two fundamental respects. For Byzantium, war with the infidel had long been a matter of every-day necessity and it had to be conducted in a realist spirit with due regard to other aspects of imperial policy. It was therefore useless to go direct to Jerusalem if this meant leaving the rear in Asia Minor inadequately protected; it might even be essential to come to terms with the Muslim if circumstances elsewhere so demanded, as for instance revolts in the Balkans, or a treacherous attack from the Normans. Further, both geography and tradition seemed to indicate that war with the infidel in Asia Minor, Syria and Palestine was the special responsibility of the East Roman Empire in particular and not of Christendom in general.

It is therefore not surprising that difficulties arose. It was only by Alexius' good management and diplomacy that the crusaders were shepherded across to Asia Minor without any major clashes. Whether unarmed pilgrims (and often rabble), or feudal contingents, they required shipping, food, guides and police, and this made considerable demands on the Byzantine countryside and resources. Doubtful of the intentions of the Latin leaders, Alexius tried to make clear his position and to safeguard it by extracting from them an oath that they would 'restore to the Roman Empire whatever towns, countries or forts they took which had formerly belonged to it'.[1] By good fortune and with the help of Byzantine guides, the crusading forces crossed Asia Minor and entered northern Syria. Their capture of Antioch in 1098 marked the parting of the ways and revealed irreconcilable aims and policies. Antioch had recently been in Byzantine hands and Alexius expected it to be handed over. But not so. It remained in the possession of Bohemund, the son of his old enemy Robert Guiscard, who set up for himself the principality of Antioch. This was followed by crusading successes elsewhere, and the establishment of the county of Edessa and the kingdom of Jerusalem, and later the county of Tripoli.

For Constantinople, the villain of the piece was Bohemund who from the moment that he appeared in its history was suspect, 'cherishing desires for the Roman Empire'. Courageous, but fickle, mischievous, malicious, Bohemund quarrelled with the other crusaders and with the Turks as well as with the Byzantines. Forced to return to the West for help, he was largely responsible for spreading the story that the Byzantines had betrayed the crusaders and he even suggested to the Pope the conquest of Constantinople itself,

1. Anna Comnena, *op. cit.*, p. 261 (X, 9).

thus fully justifying Byzantine suspicions. Bohemund attacked Greek territory in 1107 but was defeated. Byzantine prestige steadily grew. Alexius held the balance in the Balkans; recognising the importance of Hungary as a factor in Balkan and Adriatic politics, he arranged to marry his son and heir John to a Hungarian princess; he was now able to organise campaigns against the Seljuks in Asia Minor.

Alexius' assets were not only statesmanship and diplomacy in his foreign policy, though he certainly excelled at playing off one power against another; his resourcefulness and his astuteness were used to equal advantage in restoring internal prosperity. An intimate picture of the Emperor at home is found in the pages of Anna Comnena. Broad and muscular with a thick beard, eloquent even though he lisped slightly over the letter 'r' and stammered a little, Alexius was a vigorous administrator. Both in his rise to the throne and afterwards he owed much to his mother, the redoubtable Anna Dalassena; she was a formidable old lady who restored law and order to palace life, instituting a rigorous time-table, including prayers and hymns and a fixed hour for breakfast, quelling mere pleasure-seekers by 'a single look'. She fades out of Anna Comnena's picture rather suddenly and a later story rumours that she came under the spell of a heretic monk of Roman origin who worshipped Satan and addressed his prayers to a small black dog. This would naturally not have been enlarged on in the *Alexiad* where the orthodoxy of the imperial household is stressed. Alexius was fully aware of the duties of his imperial office, including the preservation of right belief.

In the stress of acute financial need Alexius had pawned 'a few church properties which served no purpose and were lying idle and neglected'; this led to somewhat strained relations until he repudiated his action. He also frequently handed over church property to be developed by laymen (this was known as a grant of *charisticum*). But on the whole he followed the traditional practice and, like his famous predecessor Constantine the Great, was anxious to root out heresy and promote religious unity in the polity. Alexius himself conducted debates with the leaders of the dualist Bogomils, with the church synod listening in, concealed behind a drawn curtain. His efforts in this direction were not entirely successful. He did rather better with erring individuals such as John Italus, an ardent student of Plato and Aristotle, who was brought to book for overstepping the bounds between pagan philosophy and Christian doctrine, like some of his contemporaries in the West.

Thus ordinary activities went on at home and Alexius' life was not exclusively occupied with war and diplomacy. His astuteness was equally revealed in his domestic policy which was necessarily much concerned with problems of finance and defence. His administration skilfully extracted the maximum from the unfortunate population, whether in the form of increased taxes or obligatory labour services. The small soldier-farmer was no longer the mainstay of the army. Mercenaries, both foreign and native, had long been used in the services and these became an increasingly important element. Use was also made of the *pronoia*, the estate granted in return for military or naval service. Earlier grants of *pronoia* which occur from the mid-eleventh century were without this obligation which appears to be first recorded in Alexius I's reign some time 'before 1119'. This kind of grantee or pronoiar was often referred to as 'the soldier' (*stratiotes*); he was equipped and mounted and accompanied by his military contingent and came from a rather different social milieu from the original small farming militia. He received the revenues of the estate, including the taxes and dues of his farming tenants. It was indeed this financial aspect which constituted one of the main attractions of the grant which at this period was usually made for life and was not alienable or heritable.

Thus Alexius chose to build on precisely those social elements which the powerful Byzantine Emperors of the middle period had tried to keep in check. His domestic and foreign policy is marked by the triumph of the military aristocracy and therein lay both its strength and its weakness. Byzantine feudalism was the product of its own internal development and was not imported from the Latin West. The western crusaders may have influenced it: the establishment of a number of Latin principalities in Palestine and Syria and the influx of Franks into the Byzantine Empire during the twelfth century was bound to familiarise the Byzantines with western feudalism. The two worlds met and each had to learn the idiom of the other. The oath of allegiance which Alexius extracted from the crusading leaders in Constantinople looked strangely like that of lord and vassal, though it had not of course the implications of the western feudal contract. Alexius accepted and made the best of new factors in imperial administration and in imperial foreign policy; his son John and his grandson Manuel had no option but to follow the lines laid down by the founder of their dynasty.

(ii) *John II Comnenus (1118–1143) and* *Manuel I Comnenus (1143–1180)*

In 1118 Alexius Comnenus died, as he had lived, surrounded by women of dominating character. But even on his death-bed he knew his own mind and refused to recognise his daughter Anna Comnena's claim to succeed him. With the succession of her hated brother and rival John, Anna's interest as a historian fades out. There is no history which makes John II the centre of its picture. He was a remarkable ruler. He was distinguished by the high moral standard of his life both in private and at court, in conversation, in appetite, in morals. His moderation and his principles were openly declared (one is reminded of his grandmother Anna Dalassena). He was equally distinguished for the prudence and tenacity with which he continued Alexius' policy; and his statesmanship was essentially that of a realist.

The twelfth century is almost spanned by the two reigns of John and his son Manuel; it is flanked at one end by the establishment of a great dynasty, representative of the military aristocratic landowning families, at the other by the swift downfall of this family and what might be called the first collapse of the Byzantine Empire. Side by side with Byzantium's fight to keep its place in the Mediterranean world was the Latin struggle to maintain its hard-won and precarious foothold in Syria and Palestine and to keep off the ring of Muslim powers which surrounded its small and isolated principalities.

A single predominating thread runs through the policies of John II and Manuel I—awareness of the dangerous ambitions of the Norman Sicilian rulers whose policy, the conquest of Constantinople, was later taken over by the German ruler Barbarossa, who strengthened his hand by marrying his heir Henry VI to the heiress of the Sicilian kingdom, Constance. The difference between John and Manuel's policies was one of emphasis and orientation, due to differences of character and circumstance. Manuel concentrated more than John on the West, on Italy in particular, but this should not blind one to the fact that both faced the same enemy and that both (despite the military disaster of 1176) scored signal successes in the East.

To some extent John's Norman problem was centred in the crusading principality of Antioch founded by Bohemund and still held by the house of Hauteville. But he also had to keep a wary eye on Sicily, and to watch carefully the moves of the other powers in the West, as well as in the Balkans and Hungary. He protected his flank in the Balkans by defeating the Patzinak raiders in 1122 for good and all; Serbia was forced to recognise his overlordship; close, if uneasy, relations were maintained with Hungary and John's first wife had been a Hungarian princess. The consolidation of the Norman power in South Italy, where Roger II was crowned king at Palermo in 1130, had alarmed both German and Byzantine rulers and they therefore drew together against their common enemy, an understanding which survived into the early years of Manuel's reign. John also approached the Papacy and in his much discussed, and as yet insufficiently elucidated, letter he mentions the two swords, which has been taken as meaning that the Pope should have the spiritual, the Roman (i.e. Byzantine) Emperor the secular, supremacy.

In the East the position of the Latin crusaders themselves was by no means secure, even without the added problem of a powerful Byzantine Emperor who wished to implement his claims to overlordship. The neighbouring Christian Armenian kingdoms in the Taurus region preserved on the whole an attitude of guarded hostility. An uneasy equilibrium was maintained between the crusading principalities, who held their own largely because the Muslim princes were at loggerheads and for the time being Constantinople was occupied elsewhere. By the thirties, however, coming ills were already casting their shadows; there were problems of succession in Jerusalem and Antioch, since in 1131 their rulers both died without male heirs, and in the north Zengi, the atabeg of Mosul, was daily growing in power. John Comnenus, moreover, used arms and diplomacy to good effect, not only among his northern and western neighbours, but in Asia Minor where he had dealt with the emirate of the Danishmends (who were at this time his main Turkish enemy rather than the Seljuks of Iconium) and had successfully taken the offensive against the kingdom of Lesser Armenia in Cilicia.

The Byzantine Emperor reached Antioch in August 1137 and triumphantly asserted his rights over its Frankish ruler, the husband of the Norman heiress. But it is significant of the underlying rifts in the Christian cause that John could never make any real advance against the infidel in northern Syria, largely for lack of Latin support. And in 1144, the year following his untimely death from a hunting wound, the Muslim Zengi captured Edessa, an event which was to provoke the unfortunate Second Crusade of 1147.

It was in such circumstances that the Byzantine crown passed to John's fourth son Manuel. Like the hero of the Byzantine epic, Digenis Akritas, the marcher lord of double race, Manuel Comnenus was of two worlds. No greater contrast could be imagined to the Emperors of earlier dynasties, a Justinian or a Constantine VII Porphyrogenitus. Manuel was a brilliant ruler, soldier and diplomat and statesman, convinced of the validity of the age-long Byzantine tradition of universal sovereignty and of the honoured imperial tradition, a devoted supporter of monasticism (in its right place) with a passion for theological discussion. And yet his mother was

Hungarian. His wives were westerners, first Bertha of Sulzbach, the sister-in-law of the German ruler Conrad, and then the fascinating Mary of Antioch. Trade, policy, political circumstances, had brought to the East Mediterranean, to the Byzantine Empire itself, a flood of westerners, many of whom had settled there. Manuel, however much he was aware of imperial Byzantium, had a great liking for the Latins and for their customs, and he is often found leading a much more informal daily life in the palace of the Blachernae in Constantinople, even himself taking part in jousts, and striking up genuine friendships with westerners, for instance King Baldwin III of Jerusalem or Conrad III of Germany; and he delighted his friends by his charm of manner and gracious hospitality (which could take a practical form, for he had considerable medical knowledge, and looked after Conrad III when he was ill in 1147). In some respects his reign thus foreshadows the Aegean world of the later middle ages.

But however partial Manuel was to Latins, his problems were in essence those of his father and grandfather—to keep off the enemies from the West. The historian Nicetas Choniates in his 7th Book has much to say on this topic and on Manuel's statesmanship. He would have been astonished to read the verdict of certain modern scholars, that 'if any one man is to be held responsible for the disaster of 1204, it is Manuel Comnenus'. He emphasises that Manuel was rightly apprehensive of the unconquered strength of the Latin nations, like the prudent farmer he tried to cut the thistles while they were still small, and he points out that Manuel's fear lest the Empire should be left without allies to face a powerful western coalition was only too well founded; once deprived of its wise pilot, i.e. Manuel, the ship of state swiftly foundered. Nicetas Choniates was writing after the catastrophe of 1204 and knew what he was talking about.

In Manuel's policy there was much that was traditional; it had however certain more unusual features which have given rise to the charge of rashness and unwise ambition, particularly in connection with his Italian designs. But it was not entirely choice that dictated the apparent western emphasis of Manuel's policy. It was essential to find some *modus vivendi* with the western powers.

Manuel began by continuing his father's alliance with Germany, but their common hostility to the Norman king could take no practical form in the West owing to the Second Crusade evoked by Bernard of Clairvaux in distress at the disintegration of the little principality of Edessa. Conrad III, Manuel's German ally, took the cross. The French crusading king Louis VII was the friend of Roger of Sicily, and it was known that these two were busy discussing the desirability of capturing Constantinople as an hors d'œuvre to their main meal further east. The crusade was however a dismal failure, partly because of perpetual quarrels and partly because its strength was directed against Damascus, usually friendly to the crusaders, instead of against Aleppo in the north where real danger threatened from one of Zengi's sons, Nur-ed-Din. By 1154 he had captured Damascus, and the death knell of the crusading kingdoms sounded when his generals Shirkuh and Saladin gained for him the strategic possession of Egypt. The hostile Muslim ring of states was soon to be controlled by a single ruler, Saladin.

During the course of the Second Crusade the Byzantine Emperor had not only to try at least to keep in touch with events in the East, but he was at the same time harassed by active Norman hostility; Greece was attacked by Roger II of Sicily, and attempts made to cause trouble in Hungary and Serbia. In spite of the Second Crusade, Manuel had kept the friendship of Conrad III and he had retaken Corfu from the Normans with Venetian help. Evidently he visualised the fulfilment of imperial policy and the countering of western intrigues in the reconquest of all, or part, of Italy. The Byzantine account of a treaty signed with Conrad at Thessalonica in 1148 states that 'the Emperor reminded him [Conrad] of those things he had previously undertaken to do, namely that he should restore Italy as her dowry to the Empress Irene[1] whom, as his kinswoman, he had betrothed to the Emperor'. This statement is not supported in western sources and its significance turns partly on the meaning of that word "Ιταλία'. Was this South Italy, or the whole of Italy?

Conrad died in 1152, and his successor Frederick I was not willing to come to terms with the Byzantine Emperor, for he thought that he himself should control Italy, including the Sicilian kingdom in the south, and in 1153 he promised Pope Eugenius III that he would not cede 'any territory' on this side of the sea to the king of the Greeks. It was therefore with the assistance of Norman rebels that Manuel began his offensive in Italy on the death of Roger II in 1154. In so doing he found a powerful circle of foes; Germany was hostile, the suspicions of Venice were roused, the Norman king William I counter-attacked, and, unable to sustain his gains in Apulia with military and naval support, his money and diplomacy were unavailing. In 1158 Byzantium signed a thirty years' truce with the Norman king. But Manuel knew who his real enemy now was; during the latter years of his reign his bitter foe was Frederick Barbarossa.

In his Italian policy of reconquest Manuel had failed. His policy

1. Bertha of Sulzbach, who was renamed Irene when she married Manuel.

roused too much opposition and his resources did not allow of any revival of the Roman Empire, and here Manuel's ambitions led him to attempt to realise an ideal which proved as impossible as that of the crusaders in Syria and Palestine. This episode was a short one and should not be exaggerated. In any case, the diplomacy which lay behind it was not without point; if Byzantium was to hold its own in the complicated network of European alliances it had to manœuvre for position and to counter enemies who for their part did not scruple to invade the Greek territory of the Empire.

In the East, by contrast, Manuel's activities were for the most part a success. Here, as in his enmity to the Normans in Italy, he continued his father's policy, but while he was hampered in the West by the growing power of Frederick Barbarossa, in the East he was helped by the failing strength of the Latin crusading principalities. As John had done, Manuel asserted his suzerainty, first over the Armenian prince in Cilicia (1158), and then proceeded to Antioch when Reynald, husband of the princess of Antioch, had to recognise Manuel's overlordship and go to his camp with a rope round his neck. Antioch's submission was the more humiliating, in that it promised Constantinople not only military aid, but the much prized and disputed right of appointing the Patriarch of the ancient see, which meant a Greek Patriarch. Manuel's entry into Antioch in 1159 made a great impression on contemporaries. He was on horseback, his horse decorated with all the imperial insignia. He was followed (at a distance) by Baldwin III who had come north and put himself under Manuel's protection, 'he hastened from Jerusalem to come to us, he acknowledged the Emperor's sovereignty'. The prince of Antioch walked beside Manuel's horse. It looked as though Byzantine overlordship might give some cohesion and unity to the Christian East and crown the patient diplomacy and military efforts of Alexius I and John II. It is an illustration of Manuel's prestige in the crusading East, that in an inscription of 1169 in the Church of the Nativity in Bethlehem, his name was given pride of place, and that of the king of Jerusalem came after it.

Manuel had similar successes on the northern frontier in Hungary, where, like his father, he sought to intervene in disputed successions to the throne, but here again he went further, and had in mind the subjugation of the whole country. He proposed a novel solution to end the long hostility between Hungary and Constantinople. The Hungarian heir Bela was to marry Manuel's daughter; he was given the title of Despot and was to succeed to the imperial throne. Thus Manuel planned to incorporate Hungary into the Empire, until his

plans were changed by the birth of his own son. He then supported
Bela's accession to the throne of Hungary, thus securing his influence
there. In Serbia he was also successful in retaining his overlordship
over the founder of a famous dynasty, the Grand Župan, Stephen
Nemanya, and celebrated this by an entry into Constantinople as
dramatic as that made earlier on into the city of Antioch.

But as Manuel's triumphs piled up, his position became more
precarious. Venice in particular had been alienated by his increased
authority in the Balkans, and by his annexation of the Dalmatian
coast, as well as by his attack on Ancona. This is reflected in
Manuel's attempt to strengthen his position by allying with Genoa
in 1169 and Pisa in 1170. Within the Empire there was sharp hostility to Venice whose trading privileges were keenly resented and a
heavy burden. More than this, feeling against the Latins was mounting. In 1171 all Venetians were arrested and their goods and ships
confiscated. War ensued and good relations were not restored until
privileges were regranted and compensation paid, probably in
Andronicus I's reign.

Manuel's successes in the Latin East and in Hungary had been
accompanied by the steady decline of his influence in the West where
he had antagonised Venice, failed to win the co-operation of the
Papacy, and had a clever and implacable enemy in Frederick Barbarossa. It was Frederick who stirred up and supported the Sultan
of Iconium against Manuel. This resulted in the crushing defeat of
Manuel in 1176 at Myriocephalum in Asia Minor. Frederick I in his
moment of exultation sent Manuel a scornful demand for the submission of the Greek king (*rex Grecorum*) to the Roman Emperor.
Frederick, announcing himself as the heir of the Roman Emperors,
claimed that this included authority over the 'regnum Greciae'. Thus
Manuel's projects had outrun his resources and proved the impossibility of maintaining authority in both Europe and the Near East
in the face of the rising western Christian states and the ring of
Muslim powers. His achievements, particularly in the field of diplomacy, were nevertheless considerable. His foreign policy, though
what might be called traditional, shows certain original features; as
for instance his attempt to conquer the old imperial possessions in
Italy by direct military action, or his remarkable project (before the
birth of his son) for uniting the thrones of Hungary and of the
Empire in the person of his son-in-law Bela, or even perhaps in his
fantastic proposal to Pope Alexander III to reconcile the Greek and
Latin Churches in return for papal support in reuniting the Empires.

But at home the economic condition of the Empire and the

growing gulf between the dependent tenant and the military ruling class, the burden of taxation, the loss of trade to foreign merchants, the depression of free men into serfdom or even slavery, were accompanied by the rapid advance of a feudalism which weakened the authority of the State. It was Manuel's brilliant personal control, indeed one might say it was the statesmanship of all three Comneni, Alexius, John and Manuel, which held together an Empire that was fast becoming an anachronism, despite its services as a buffer-state and as the home of a distinguished civilisation.

3. THE FIRST COLLAPSE

With the disappearance of Manuel I's forceful and attractive personality and the accession of a minor, his son Alexius II, the strength of certain underlying trends in twelfth-century Byzantine life became obvious. The Latin menace took the form, not of attacks from without, but of an insidious internal penetration. Byzantium was flooded with Latins of all kinds—hangers-on, genuine traders, members of the western feudal families bound by ties of blood or friendship to the Byzantine court. It was equally clear that under the Comnenian régime the power of the landed families had been enormously strengthened, partly due to their steady acquisition of land granted them in *pronoia*, which usually carried with it additional financial and jurisdictional rights. This system of granting out land was so widespread in the Empire by 1204 that westerners on their conquered lands felt quite at home, and Byzantines in Greece for their part had no difficulty in understanding their position as vassals of their Latin overlords.

Manuel Comnenus had been a popular ruler, moving freely among Greek and Latin alike, but he was powerless to stay the rising tide of anti-Latin feeling or the steady diminution of central authority. On his death the weakness of the Byzantine Empire was as obvious as that of the Latin crusading principalities in Syria and Palestine. Both virtually collapsed within a short time of each other, though for different reasons, the one falling to the Christian West, the other to the powerful Muslim enemy, Saladin.

The rule of a minor with an unpopular Latin mother very quickly ended with the murder of both by Manuel's cousin Andronicus I. He had never seen eye to eye with Manuel and had led a restless life wandering round the courts of the Near East. Unconventional and fascinating, his charm had lured Theodora Comnena, the widow of Baldwin III of Jerusalem, to elope with him, and as an old man (he was sixty-five when he came to the throne) he could win the affection and sympathy of the little thirteen-year-old French Agnes-Anna whom he married after killing her boy husband Alexius II. Andronicus had the courage of his convictions and he reverted to the policy of the middle Byzantine period, but not even a Basil II could have succeeded at the end of the twelfth century, and Andronicus had none of Basil's patience or self-control. His policy was to purify the administration, to root out the Latin elements in the Empire and to strengthen the central authority by curtailing the power of the military aristocracy. But any elements of statesmanship were swamped by his tempestuous and violent methods. Before he entered Constantinople, there had already been a terrible and indiscriminate mob attack on all foreigners in the City, 'the accursed Latins'. Andronicus instituted a vigorous clean-up of central and provincial administration; his working principle was said to be 'If you do not cease from mal-administration, you can cease from living.' Grants of privilege to the great land-owners had gone too far for recall, and going in fear of his life, he chose to resort to violence. His stand against the great families took the form of wholesale execution and extermination, thus robbing the Empire of military leaders whose services it badly needed.

Andronicus' policy only antagonised both the western powers with whom it was essential to come to terms and the landed aristocracy who alone had the resources with which the State could be defended. Hungary attacked and took Dalmatia, and parts of Croatia and Sirmium; Stephen Nemanya of Serbia (Rašca and Zeta) renounced his allegiance; the Norman Sicilians occupied Corfu and other Greek islands and then advanced to sack Thessalonica (1185). Within the Empire, the extremes to which the hostility of the landed magnates could go were evidenced by a member of the Comnenian family, Isaac, who set himself up as the independent ruler of Cyprus, a clear instance of the latent separatist tendencies in Byzantium which came to the surface during and after the Fourth Crusade.

Andronicus' reign of terror and the news that the victorious Normans were advancing on the capital brought about the final downfall of the Comnenian dynasty in 1185. From 1185 to 1204 the throne was held by rulers of the Angeli house, none of them possessing the statesmanship of a John or a Manuel Comnenus, though they were by no means nonentities. But the old abuses crept back into the government. By now the themes had greatly increased in number, though they were only shrunken versions of the former powerful administrative units. The decisive factor was now the great private estate and the estate held in *pronoia*. The authority of the powerful landlord was rapidly ousting the provincial governor, thus foreshadowing the late medieval development of virtually independent principalities or appanages.

In the North, Byzantium failed to quell rising national and separatist feeling in Bulgaria, since 1018 incorporated into the Empire. An independent kingdom, the Second Bulgarian Empire, was set up by local magnates, probably of Bulgaro-Wallachian descent, calling themselves 'imperatores' of the whole of Bulgaria and Wallachia. They found support from many elements of discontent. They themselves had been originally provoked in 1185 by being refused certain grants in *pronoia*. The *pronoia* is seen here not as an expression of feudal tendencies but of centrifugal forces. And it may be noted that these grants were being made not only to Byzantine landlords, or to Latin feudal lords as the Montferrat family, but to such as the Cumans in the Balkans whose wealth was primarily in herds and flocks and not land. The Byzantine Emperor Isaac II Angelus failed to crush the revolt and Asen was crowned Bulgarian 'Emperor' by the newly established archbishop of Trnovo in 1187. Here in the Balkans was further evidence of the disintegration within the Empire and of the power of the local magnates.

The Latin menace took a double form. The Norman invaders of 1185 again invaded Greece and even sacked Thessalonica. They were expelled from the mainland, for the Empire was not entirely without military resources, but they kept the islands of Cephalonia and Zacynthus. In addition, danger threatened from another crusade. Weakened by recent civil war and by military campaigns in the Balkans and Greece and ruled by an Emperor of only moderate ability, in 1189 Byzantium had to face the approaching Third Crusade occasioned by the fall of Jerusalem in 1187.

Since the Second Crusade of 1147 the position in the Latin Orient had steadily deteriorated. The kingdom of Jerusalem, after a series of brilliant leaders, had failed to establish a stable dynasty, while constant clashes between Byzantine and Latin, as well as among the Latins themselves, had made it impossible to follow up hardly won advantages. The situation was not retrieved by a crusade led by three kings of western Europe, though Richard I of England, a superb soldier and on occasion an astute statesman, was able to sign a treaty with Saladin in 1192 salvaging a small strip of coast including Acre and Tyre and gaining access to the Holy Places for Christians. For the Byzantines, the journey of the crusaders whether by sea or land was of ill-omen. The Germans came through the

C

Balkans and the hostility of their leader Frederick Barbarossa, the implacable enemy of the Byzantines, led to so tense a situation that at one point the Pope was asked to bless a crusade against the Byzantine Empire. Frederick's unexpected death in Asia Minor in 1190 gave Byzantium a temporary respite. Richard of England went by sea with equally disastrous consequences for Constantinople. He captured Cyprus from Isaac Comnenus. Thus the island, already lost to the central government, passed from Greek into Latin hands.

The failure of the Third Crusade recoiled on Byzantium. Difficulties in the way of maintaining even what was left of the crusading kingdoms in Syria and Palestine were obvious and the Latins reconsidered their tactics and looked elsewhere. The conception of a crusade against the infidel was so ingrained in the contemporary Christian world that any frank and open abandonment of the struggle would have been unthinkable. Specious arguments and obvious material advantages could however be put forward in support of an attack on Byzantium as the first step to a really effective offensive. In the West it had long been usual to impute crusading failures to the alleged hostility of the supposedly perfidious Byzantines.

The lead now came from the German ruler, Barbarossa's son. Henry VI was the heir of the Sicilian Normans in more senses than one. By marriage he had succeeded to their territorial possessions and by the end of 1194 had overcome opposition and been crowned in Palermo. By instinct and tradition he inclined towards their eastern policy, which in western imperial hands took on a more ambitious form, nothing less than the domination of Christendom. The preliminary step was the conquest, or at any rate the subjugation, of Byzantium. The overthrow of Isaac II in 1195, whose daughter had married Henry's brother Philip, gave him some pretext for intervening and he demanded a stiff tribute of gold, called in Byzantium the 'German' tax. In the Near East Henry was already preparing the way for a fresh crusade: he had obtained recognition of his overlordship from Cyprus and from Lesser Armenia. But his plans were cut short by his death in 1197. This deprived the crusading cause of a leader who seemed capable of giving it unity and direction: it did not save Constantinople.

IV

THE IMPACT OF EAST AND WEST
1204–1453

1. LATIN TREACHERY AND BYZANTINE DIPLOMACY
1204–1261

The Fourth Crusade had Egypt as its preliminary objective, but it was diverted, first to Zara, a Christian city on the Dalmatian coast to which Venice considered it had more claim than its rival Hungary, and then to Constantinople, ostensibly in order to restore to the throne the deposed Angeli rulers. This diversion of the crusade to the capital of the Byzantine Empire is not difficult to account for: the wonder is that it had not occurred before. Venice, jealous of its Italian rivals in the East, wished to secure its own trade and resented recent Byzantine attempts to restrict its extensive privileges. Other powers in the West also resented the violent outbursts of anti-Latin feeling. In addition the legend that the Byzantines had been responsible throughout for crusading misfortunes had taken deep root. The capture of Constantinople was not a new idea and it now seemed particularly opportune and attractive. From the outset a strongly secular element had been present in the western crusading movement and it was clear that the Byzantine Empire now offered a more lucrative and a safer field for Latin colonisation than Palestine and Syria. In the long run the capture of Constantinople and the partial dismemberment of the Byzantine Empire had disastrous effects on the crusading cause. It diverted western crusaders from Palestine and Syria. More important still, it meant a hardening of the rift between eastern and western Christendom, thus aggravating a dissension in the Christian ranks which greatly weakened future resistance to a more dangerous infidel enemy, the Ottoman Turk.

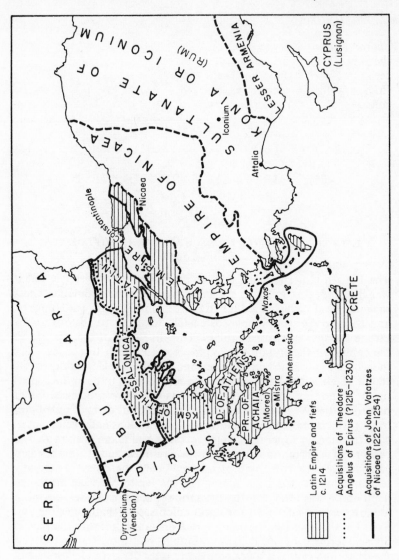

The Aegean World *c.* 1214–1254
(after Ostrogorsky)

The Fourth Crusade ruthlessly exploited the difficulties of the Angeli Emperors who were quite unable to keep their promises of financial and military help. Constantinople was forcibly captured by the Latin Christians. It was then sacked, and the 'crusaders' proceeded to divide the capital and indeed the rest of the Byzantine Empire amongst themselves, and they set off on the systematic conquest of their newly allotted spoils. As the result, a Latin Empire and a number of Latin principalities came into being. Within a short time the Latins controlled Thrace, Thessalonica, the greater part of Greece and many of the islands in the Aegean. They were divided among themselves, at cross purposes over territorial claims and commercial privileges and often, in the early days at any rate, pursuing a policy at variance with the more conciliatory wishes of the Holy See. They could offer no effective substitute for the autocratic rule of a single Emperor and during the course of the later middle ages their lands were gradually absorbed by their various neighbours, in particular, the Serbs, the Byzantines and the Ottoman Turks.

But the Latins were a factor in the Aegean world for almost two hundred and fifty years. Bitter political rivalry was accompanied by fruitful personal contacts, by mutual interest in their respective civilisations and by inevitable cross-fertilisation. In the thirteenth century Frankish courts, particularly at Athens, Thebes and in the Peloponnese, enjoyed a short-lived but brilliant life. The new rulers attempted on the whole to deal reasonably with their conquered subjects; many Greek land-owners continued to hold their property, but as vassals of their western lords. The feudal system, as understood by the West, was transplanted to Greece. The captured French ruler of the Peloponnese, William of Villehardouin (†1278), had to explain to the Byzantine Emperor that he could pay a ransom, but could not alienate his vassals' lands. 'My Lord Emperor, if I stayed in your prison a thousand years I could not alter the position. The Morea was conquered by force of arms . . . by my father and his companions, other brave men of France, and they ruled amongst themselves, according to law and custom, that the land should pass to their heirs.'[1] The fortresses which William finally handed over to Michael VIII were his own conquests (as Mistra or Monemvasia). Though the larger principalities were short-lived, the Latins kept, or acquired, a number of economic bases which were invaluable either as transit depots or by reason of their products. For instance the

1. *Chronicle of the Morea*, Greek version ed. J. Schmitt (London 1904), verses 4255–4301; French version ed. J. Longnon (Paris 1911), pp. 116–17; English translation by H. E. Lurier (Columbia Univ. Press 1964).

valuable alum mines at Phocaea at the entrance to the gulf of Smyrna were granted to the Genoese in 1275, and the Gattilusii made fortunes out of them. Thebes and the Morea were famous for their silk industry as well as for their silk-yarn. The Venetian family of the Sanudi established themselves on Naxos and extended their control over the neighbouring islands, carefully nursing the trade in that area.

Thus on the whole the Latin conquest tended to stimulate economic activity: it was in the conqueror's own interests to promote prosperous trade and was indeed one of the prime motives for the attack on the Empire. Too often diplomatic intrigues and dynastic struggles obscure comparatively peaceful everyday activities, which depended for their very existence on some measure of mutual understanding between Greek and Latin.

When the Byzantine capital fell in 1204 after a continuous existence of over eight centuries, the Empire split into two Greek principalities. The kingdom of Epirus was established in north-west Greece, consisting of Epirus and part of Albania under the rule of Theodore Angelus, and the kingdom of Nicaea in north-west Asia Minor under Theodore Lascaris, who had married into the Angeli family. On the south-east shores of the Black Sea there was also the Greek kingdom of Trebizond under a branch of the Comnenian family. This last had in fact been set up with the support of Georgia before the conquest of Constantinople. These principalities, though in part occasioned by the events of 1204, also reflected the separatist tendencies amongst the powerful Byzantine families. The despotate of Epirus and the kingdom of Nicaea both claimed to have inherited the imperial mantle. The third competitor for the imperial throne was the able Bulgarian ruler John II Asen (1218–1241). All three struggled to substantiate their claim by enlarging their boundaries and gaining possession of Constantinople either by force or by diplomacy.

Bulgaria however dropped out of the race after the death of John Asen. Epirus was weakened by dynastic difficulties and to its disadvantage became involved with its Latin neighbours. Nicaea was for a number of reasons the victor. In actual fact it was a stronger and more compact little kingdom than the Empire which had been broken up. The Lascarid dynasty was astute and enlightened: its rulers carefully husbanded and nursed their internal resources and found time to encourage cultural activities. At the same time they turned the mistakes of their rivals to their own advantage. They had at any rate the temporary support of the Seljuk Turks of Iconium and the Greek rulers of Trebizond, both of whom were feeling the repercussions of the Mongolian movements which were in process of altering the political configuration of the Middle East. Working from their strong base in Asia Minor, the Lascarids cleverly re-established themselves in Europe, in Macedonia and Thrace and in Thessalonica. When Theodore II Lascaris died in 1258, leaving a minor, the issue was decided by the 'urbane and courteous', but un-scrupulous, Michael Palaeologus, who was sufficiently able to reap the benefit of the Lascarids' work. He crushed a coalition of Epirus, Manfred of Sicily and the Franks of the Morea at the battle of Pelagonia in 1259. He tried to make sure of a powerful maritime ally against Venice, the instigator and chief beneficiary of the Fourth Crusade, by allying in March 1261 with the Genoese who were given valuable trading privileges in return for promised help. Then on 25 July 1261 the City was captured, and a few days later Michael VIII made his solemn entry, going on foot to the Studite monastery of St John and thence to the church of Hagia Sophia. His house ruled the revived Byzantine Empire from Constantinople for nearly two hundred years until the final Ottoman conquest in the fifteenth century.

2. CHRISTIAN RIVALRIES AND BYZANTINE CIVIL WARS 1261–1354

During its very precarious existence the Empire of the Palaeologi varied in territorial extent. In 1261 it had north-west Asia Minor and most of Thrace and Macedonia, certain of the islands and control over Epirus, as well as four key fortresses in what was still Frankish Greece. Although it managed to extend its territory after 1261, particularly in the Peloponnese, it was never able to nurse back to life any effective system of government centred in Con-stantinople. Again and again it had to resort to the expedient of what was virtually an appanage system. Instead of themes adminis-tered by governors responsible to, and under, the control of the central authority, a series of provinces or appanages are found, usually granted out to members either of the imperial house or the co-Emperor's family. Constantinople itself still had great prestige, and was a factor to be reckoned with in international politics: geo-graphy alone ensured this. There was still wealth within the Empire, but it was not in imperial hands. It was controlled by the important families and the great ecclesiastical foundations, and by now grants of land originally made in *pronoia* in return for service were often made heritable and free of conditions. This change in the *pronoia* system had its effect on the army which was by now almost entirely mercenary and was consequently a heavy expense. At the same time the fleet was practically non-existent and Constantinople relied on Genoese help. Byzantine sailors who found themselves out of work would sign on with Turkish pirates who were a scourge in the Aegean and particularly round the coastal districts of Asia Minor. The imperial exchequer received only an infinitesimal fraction of its former receipts. Sometimes the local farmers and peasants were reduced to poverty by the ravages of war and could not pay up; more often local revenue was collected by the magnate of the district. A former lucrative source of income, the customs dues and tolls, now went for the most part into the pockets of the Italians, particularly the Genoese within the Byzantine territory, while the bezant, the Byzantine gold piece, which used to be the coin of international trade, was superseded by 'the good money' of the Italian republics.

The problem of the Byzantine government after 1261 was, then, one of diminished and totally inadequate material resources. Without the backing of proper military and naval defence it found that diplomacy alone was of no avail; unable to enforce its authority within its own territory, it had no option but to suffer, and in the end to rely on, the virtually independent land-owners and local governors. Internal difficulties such as these were increased by long periods of civil war during the fourteenth century and by the continuous pressure from without from 1261 onwards, particularly from Charles of Anjou, from Serbia, and finally from the Ottoman Turks.

For a short time the deceptive brilliance of Michael VIII disguised the essential weakness of the restored Empire. He neatly staved off a dangerous situation by adroit diplomacy. Charles of Anjou had recently established himself in the kingdom of Sicily, where he had defeated the Hohenstaufen in 1266. Charles wished to extend his authority to Greece and the Byzantine Empire, and he built up an alliance against Michael VIII. He was supported by the Papacy and the former Latin Emperor of Constantinople, Baldwin II, and William of Villehardouin (who had been defeated by Michael VIII in the Morea)—clearly a dangerous alliance. The Byzantine Emperor cleverly used the Golden Horde and the Mongol Khan Hulagu against Bulgaria and Rum, and Hungary against Serbia, thus countering his enemies in Asia Minor and the Balkans. He held out the advantages of a friendly alliance to Charles' brother Louis IX, who was contemplating a crusade. He subsidised the

Sicilians who were bitterly hostile to their Angevin ruler, with the result that they successfully revolted and gave the crown to Peter of Aragon with whom he came to an understanding. He also thought it wise to win over the Papacy with the promise of ecclesiastical reunion at the Council of Lyons in 1274.

Michael thus broke up Charles' plans, but at great cost, both financially and in other respects. His approach to Rome roused bitter opposition in neighbouring orthodox countries, for instance Bulgaria, where there was strong feeling against Constantinople. It was equally bitterly opposed at home. When mass was celebrated in the imperial chapel in Constantinople on 9 January 1275 the epistle and gospel were chanted in both Greek and Latin, and commemoration made of Gregory, 'the chief Pontiff of the apostolic Church and oecumenical Pope'. But the feeling of one and all was voiced by the Emperor's sister, who is reported to have said, 'Better that my brother's Empire should perish than the purity of the Orthodox faith.' This offer of union between Rome and Constantinople became a well-worn imperial gambit during the Palaeologan period, but after 1204 many Byzantines preferred submission to the infidel rather than the abandonment of what they regarded as the long venerated traditions of their Church. And as their enemies closed in, the Byzantines clung all the more to the Orthodox Church whose authority and prestige steadily increased.

The international position won under Michael VIII could not be sustained. This was not because of the ineffectiveness of individual Byzantine rulers some of whom, as John Cantacuzenus or Manuel II, were certainly outstanding and gifted men, but was due to the impossibility of restoring firm central control in the face of increasing feudal separatism and to the complete lack of adequate resources with which to counter the Serbian enemy in the Balkans and the Ottoman enemy in Asia Minor. Within the Empire cultural activities and religious controversy flourished, despite its perilous situation. As always in Byzantium, there were hot disputes between different church parties, often allied to different political factions, and in the fourteenth century there was the added complication of keenly felt and widely expressed social and economic grievances, particularly in the city of Thessalonica, where for several years in the mid-fourteenth century government (if it can be called such) was by the people's committee. There were rivalries at a higher level. The old Emperor Andronicus II (1282–1328) came to loggerheads with his grandson and heir Andronicus III who raised an army against him. When Andronicus III died in 1341 a second civil war broke out between the Grand Domestic John Cantacuzenus and the regency. An uneasy *modus vivendi* was achieved by the coronation of Cantacuzenus as John VI by the Patriarch of Constantinople in 1347, followed by the steady increase in the power of his family. Meanwhile the resentment of the young Emperor John V Palaeologus grew and with the help of the Genoese he forced Cantacuzenus to abdicate in 1354. But even though the Emperor John Cantacuzenus became the monk Joasaph and spent much of his time writing a history and theological works, he still continued to intervene in affairs of church and state until his death in 1383.

The disunity within the Empire inevitably hampered any attempt to extend its diminished territory, and outside rivals quickly seized the opportunity of playing off one Byzantine party against the other. In the fourteenth century Byzantium had most to fear from the Serbs in the Balkans and the Ottoman Turks in Asia Minor. Serbia had learnt much from the older civilisation of its near neighbour and under the capable Nemanići rulers it began to take a vigorous and leading part in Balkan politics, particularly during the reign of Stephen Dušan (1331–1355). At the height of Dušan's power Serbia had successfully exploited the civil war between John V Palaeologus and John Cantacuzenus, and had profited by Venice's fear of Hungary's ambitions. Stephen Dušan felt strong enough to dream of supplanting the Palaeologi, and he hoped to restore the prosperity of the Roman Empire. In addition to the lands originally occupied by the Serbian tribes, his territory had been expanded to include Albania, Epirus, Thessaly and Macedonia (though he never occupied the important city of Thessalonica), while Bulgaria was virtually a vassal state. When he wrote to the Doge in 1345 he called himself 'lord of almost all the Roman Empire'. For a time he had allied with John Cantacuzenus; then he turned against John because he feared his growing strength. Stephen Dušan died at the height of his power in 1355 before he had been able to attack Constantinople or lead a crusade against the Turks. It is doubtful whether his efforts could have had any lasting success, for his kingdom was as yet not sufficiently developed to sustain the burden of Empire or to consolidate its newly acquired lands. Thus the Balkan states in the later middle ages were too powerful to be re-incorporated into the revived Byzantine Empire, but not one of them was strong enough to impose any measure of unity on the discordant elements in the Christian world in the Balkans and the Aegean.

3. THE TURKISH CONQUEST AND THE FINAL COLLAPSE OF BYZANTIUM 1354–1453

The old Turkish enemies in Asia Minor had been the Seljuk kingdom of Konia (or Rum) and the emirate of the Danishmends. In the course of the thirteenth century this situation was changed by the Mongol advance. The sultanate of Konia disappeared as an effective political entity and in western Asia Minor, taking advantage of Byzantine concentration on European affairs, a number of small emirates were formed. To begin with, most of these were Ghazi in tradition;[1] they were peopled by the marcher lords of the Muslim world whose warriors fought for the faith. They attacked the Byzantine provinces in Asia Minor, and their pirate fleets infested the Aegean waters, often reinforced by unemployed Byzantine sailors. In the north-west, occupying part of the old Byzantine Bithynia, was the emirate of Osman. It enjoyed a strategic position commanding routes from Constantinople to Asia. The Ottomans were therefore well-placed for future raids on Europe. They were also brought into contact with the old Islamic administrative and cultural traditions of the hinterland, so that they did not remain simply a Ghazi frontier state but they developed foundations on which an empire could be built.

Both Christian and Muslim powers were accustomed to ally with each other according to the needs of the moment. By the mid-fourteenth century the Ottoman emirate had established its position in Asia Minor and when John VI Cantacuzenus needed help against John Palaeologus during the civil war he turned to Orchan, its ruler. He gave Orchan his daughter in marriage and was aided in Thrace by a strong contingent of Ottoman troops. Until his abdication in 1354, Cantacuzenus was supported by these Turks. Their participation in the Byzantine civil wars on European soil marked the beginning of their settlement in Europe. In 1354 they had occupied Gallipoli and from their base they began their systematic conquest of the Balkans.

After the abdication of John VI in 1354, John V Palaeologus forced Cantacuzenus' son Matthew Cantacuzenus to renounce his claims, but wisely agreed to recognise another son as ruler in the Morea. During the rest of his long reign—he died in 1391—his major problem was how to stave off the Ottoman advance in the Balkans. The resources of the Byzantine crown were clearly inadequate and

1. A Ghazi was the special champion of the religion of Allah.

in any case the most flourishing part of the Empire, the Morea, was
virtually an independent principality. John therefore attempted to
gain help from the West. Unfortunately the first requisite now, as
earlier, was an understanding with the Papacy and the union of the
churches of Rome and Constantinople. A few clear-sighted Byzantines realised the need for this, but the majority, fully supported by
the powerful Greek Orthodox Church, remained obstinately opposed to such a policy. John's proposals of 1355 were therefore
fruitless: no effective help came from the Pope and the Byzantines
refused to consider ecclesiastical reunion. Pressed still further,
John V journeyed as a suppliant to the court of Hungary but failed
again because of the ecclesiastical rift. Still hoping for crusading
assistance and spurred on by his cousin, the Count of Savoy, who
had arrived in 1366, John (whose mother had been a Latin) then
went himself to Rome and in October 1369 was converted to the
Roman faith, while his Patriarch was simultaneously exhorting the
Byzantines and the Orthodox of other countries firmly to resist any
such move.

Meanwhile the Ottomans under Murad I (1362–1389) extended
their European territory at the expense of both Serbia and Byzantium, and their present success and future intentions were
symbolised by the Sultan's transference of his court from Asia
Minor to Thrace. From about 1365 onwards it was established in
Adriancple. While John V was vainly wandering round Europe and
pledging himself to the Roman Church, the Ottomans were moving
into Macedonia. The Serbs, now split into various principalities,
were seriously defeated in 1371, and were finally crushed on the
plain of Kosovo in 1389 (the battle of the Field of Blackbirds). They
had to submit and do military service and pay tribute. Bulgaria had
to recognise Turkish overlordship. Thus Byzantium was virtually a
Turkish dependency and its Emperor little more than a vassal who
was liable for military service.

The Byzantine Empire was able to struggle on until the mid-
fifteenth century, mainly for two reasons: Constantinople was an
almost impregnable fortress, and the Ottomans had a totally unexpected set-back in Asia Minor in 1402. During this time it was
clear that Byzantium had lost its former standing in international
politics: hopelessly reduced in territorial extent and no longer able
to control even a fraction of such wealth as remained in Greek
hands; continually rent by strife within the imperial family where
John's son Andronicus IV was perpetually opposing his father; involved in the bitter rivalry of the two Italian republics Venice and

Genoa who controlled important interests in the East; and at the same time bound by necessity to respect the wishes of its powerful suzerain, the Ottoman Sultan—it is surprising that the Empire maintained even a shadow existence for so long.

Except for its territory in the Morea, the Empire really only consisted of Constantinople. Here from 1391 to 1425 Manuel II ruled. According to the Byzantine historian Ducas, the Ottoman Sultan said to Manuel, 'Close the gates of the city and rule within it, for I own everything outside the walls.' Sure of himself, the Sultan Bayezid began to bring pressure to bear: Constantinople was virtually blockaded; Thessaly was captured in 1393 and the Ottomans now began to penetrate further south into the Morea. Bulgaria, already a vassal state, was occupied—its capital Trnovo fell in 1393. The Dobrudja was taken, and the Danube was under Turkish control. The penetration into Greece although it affected Italian, as well as Byzantine, interests might have left Latin Europe unmoved; but the subjugation of Bulgaria and the approach to the Danube was a dangerous threat to Hungary where King Sigismund succeeded in mustering crusading help from various western sources. This Christian force was crushed at Nicopolis in 1396, and the Turks continued to advance in Greece.

At this point Manuel II, like his father before him, set out to travel round the courts of the Latin world organising an appeal for help—not indeed to recapture Jerusalem, but to save the city that had for so long stood as the eastern bulwark of Christendom. Everywhere Manuel's cruel plight and his imperial bearing roused sympathy. Even Adam of Usk in 'the far-off isles of the west' lamented 'the fallen glory of Rome'. But nothing tangible was done and Manuel must have realised the indifference of western rulers. Then the news reached him that the Ottoman Sultan Bayezid had stirred the anger of the Mongol ruler Timur by his ambitions on the eastern borders of his emirate. After Nicopolis, Bayezid had gone East towards the Euphrates, visualising a universal Muslim empire. Such ambitions roused Timur who considered his appearance in the East Muslim world a menace. Timur attacked the Ottoman and decisively defeated him at Ankara in 1402. Bayezid was captured and civil war broke out in the Ottoman emirate. But Byzantium and the other Christian principalities were either too weak or else too disunited to take full advantage of their enemy's downfall. Instead of putting up a common and united front, they themselves tried to further their individual interests by taking sides in the Ottoman struggles. When Mohammed I had defeated his rivals, he devoted his reign to internal consolidation, and this gave the Byzantine Empire a breathing space. Manuel was on good terms with his enemy and the two would chat together and exchange courtesies from their imperial barges in the Bosphorus. Mistra in the Morea was the stronghold of all that remained of Byzantine civilisation and its scholars and thinkers stressed the value of its Hellenic tradition. It is noticeable that at this time when their existence was so precarious, the Byzantines in the Morea called themselves 'Hellenes', and not 'Romaioi' as they had formerly done. But it was to be several centuries before Greek national feeling was able to find expression in an independent political entity.

Mohammed I's successor Murad II made clear his intention of taking Constantinople. Now for the last time the Byzantine Emperor journeyed to Italy and on this occasion even persuaded the Patriarch of Constantinople and some of the Greek clergy to accompany him. In 1439 the union of the two Churches was proclaimed in Greek and in Latin in the Duomo in Florence where a general church council was being held. Far from securing practical help, this only enraged the Byzantine people and estranged the Slav Orthodox, particularly Russia. In the Balkans the last stand was made. The king of Hungary, the Serbian George Branković and John Hunyadi of Transylvania entered the Balkans in 1443. They were supported by the Albanian leader Scanderbeg. Murad II tried first of all to divide his opponents by negotiating a treaty with them in 1444. Stirred up by the Papacy, Hungary broke the truce and marched towards the Black Sea, only to be wiped out at the battle of Varna.

In 1448 Constantine XI, the last Byzantine Emperor, succeeded to the throne. His two brothers ruled in the Morea, and he himself was master of the capital. The Byzantines, even with the Ottoman Mohammed II at their gates, still hated any compromise with Rome; in Ducas' often quoted words, they would rather see the Muslim turban in the centre of the City than the Latin mitre. Some of the Genoese supported their ally to the end, and, with the courageous Emperor, died fighting. The Byzantines had nothing that could stand up to the modern Turkish artillery—the enemy had only to batter long enough at the fortifications; the Christians could not repair the breaches and the first janissaries successfully scaled the walls on 29 May 1453. The Ottoman had four almost unanswerable weapons: superior military technique; ample financial resources; the disunity of the Christian princes; and the internal condition of the Byzantine Empire.

The possessions in the Morea and the kingdom of Trebizond survived only for a few years, and by the end of the century almost all of the old Byzantine Empire was in Muslim hands. Once again an Empire stood from the Euphrates to the Danube. Different elements in the Muslim world interpreted this in different ways: to some it was the work of the Ghazis, the warriors of the faith; to others it was the realisation of the aspirations of Old Islam. For the Christian world much had been destroyed, but much remained. The magnificently rebuilt city was a centre not only for Muslims but also for Christians. It was still the headquarters of the Patriarch. The Orthodox Church had now become the only guardian of the cultural and religious life of the subject Slavs and Greeks, and throughout the Ottoman Empire Christians found their one outlet in their local parish community. In post-Byzantine days, the Church had to do without the Emperor and to rely upon itself.

V

CHURCH AND STATE:

THE IMPERIAL GOVERNMENT

The Byzantine Empire was indissolubly linked with the *imperium romanum* of Late Antiquity. It inherited a tradition containing not only Roman, but strong Hellenistic and eastern elements which were taken for granted by both the Roman and Byzantine worlds. This accounts for much in the medieval East Roman Empire which has often been described as 'orientalisation' of an almost contemporary date. Byzantium was no doubt influenced by frequent direct contact with its eastern neighbours, but certain prominent eastern features in its conception of imperial authority were inherited from Rome, though in origin they derived from traditions stretching far back into the other civilisations of the ancient world—Hellenistic, Persian, Assyrian, Babylonian, Hebrew and Egyptian. By the third century A.D. the government of the Graeco-Roman world was monarchical and absolute, its ruler was closely associated with divinity and the claim to a universal Empire. Old Rome had indeed travelled far from its republican days. It had become the capital city of an Emperor who was the shepherd, benefactor and saviour of his people, to whom divine honours were paid. With the recognition of Christianity still further changes were introduced. In the course of the fourth century the Roman Empire had come first to tolerate Christianity, then to adopt it as the state religion. This recognition of the claims of Christianity chiefly affected its government in two ways—current Hellenistic conceptions of imperial authority had to be reconsidered and restated in the light of Christian belief and thought, and then the Christian Church, with its own special needs and with its claims on each individual, had to be fitted into the framework of the body politic.

As far as imperial authority was concerned it was not difficult to bridge the gulf, and early medieval conceptions reflect the Hellenistic idiom and ancestry. The Emperor could no longer be regarded as divine, but, and this was almost the same for practical purposes, he was looked upon as being divinely appointed by God to be His representative on earth. As there was one God, so there was one Emperor, who would in the fulness of time have world domination, universal rule. Byzantine literature and Byzantine customs abundantly illustrate this close connection between God and His ruler. In contrast to St Augustine's view of the two cities and the perpetual pilgrimage, the whole history of the Byzantine Empire bears out the fourth-century Eusebius' view that Christianity was to transform the earthly Empire. To the Byzantines it appeared fitting to liken the imperial responsibilities to those of St Peter. 'Since God handed over to us the sovereignty of the Empire, as was His good pleasure He also . . . commanded us, as He commanded Peter the supreme head of the apostles, to feed His most faithful flock.'[1]

The Emperor was surrounded by ceremonial that was religious in character and was closely connected with the ecclesiastical liturgy. The left side of the imperial throne was dedicated to Christ, and was left vacant on great occasions such as the church festivals, but was occupied by the Emperor, as Christ's representative on earth, when he was receiving ambassadors. Light, fire and incense were carried before him on certain occasions, and it was usual to cense him in church. Above all, his place in both religious and secular life was shown by the acclamations which were accorded him. These acclamations were something like solemn hymns (a near equivalent is our 'God Save the Queen', which is a series of acclamations). They stressed the position of the Emperor as God's direct representative and he was greeted in this way on all festal occasions, whether in the hippodrome or in Hagia Sophia. The Whitsun festal hymns speak of the Holy Ghost in the form of fiery tongues settling on the Emperor, the acclamations on Christmas Eve are linked with the hymns and lessons appointed for that season. 'May Christ the source of all life support your rule, and, your majesty, may He move nations throughout the universe to offer tributes to your royal power, as the Magi offered presents to Him.' These anthems were sung by special choirs, some ecclesiastical, some provided by the old political city guilds. There is a wealth of detail about the procedure of the imperial court to be found in the *Book of Ceremonies* which was compiled by Constantine VII in the tenth century. The inscription and introduction show the connection of the Byzantine Emperor with

1. *Ecloga*, Preface.

Christ, he is the φιλοχριστός, the friend of Christ. It is carefully explained that ceremonial is valued because it symbolises that good order in the Empire which reflects the divine harmony with which the Creator has endowed the whole universe.

The Byzantine Emperor, who regarded himself as the heir of Constantine the Great, the thirteenth apostle, was in theory elected, but in practice he might be chosen by various methods. The Emperor-elect could be designated by the reigning Emperor during his lifetime, or he might seize control after eliminating or deposing the reigning Emperor, or he might assume authority as co-Emperor. He was normally acclaimed by the people, the senate, and the army, of whom the army was probably the most important element. The fact that he was successful was regarded as a sign of divine support, and the Byzantines were accustomed to accept what came. God in His wisdom might not always provide good rulers. There is a passage in the *Spuria Athanasiana* in which God is asked why He allowed such a monster as Phocas to become Emperor at the beginning of the seventh century. He replies, 'Because I could not find anyone worse.' That is of course exceptional—mankind was not usually put to such extreme tests of faith and endurance. From the seventh century onwards there was a steady growth of the hereditary principle and one or more sons of the reigning Emperor were normally crowned during his lifetime. The existence of more than one, or perhaps several, co-Emperors did not break the unity of imperial rule. This practice went back to the days of the principate when Augustus had a daughter and no sons. The habit of association safeguarded the succession, or it might also be used to give authority to a strong adult ruler in times of minority, or to secure effective government when the heir of the imperial house was a woman or a man who lacked qualities of statesmanship. There might be many Emperors, there was only one ruler, the senior Autocrator, who was from the early seventh century known as the Basileus. After the imperial coronation of the western Charles the Great, the Byzantine Emperor was styled Basileus Romaion, 'Emperor of the Romans', thus emphasising the claim to universal rule as the heir of Rome. The title of Autocrator (which was a translation of Imperator) came to be used only for the senior Emperor. It was not until the later middle ages that the first of the co-Emperors, as distinct from the senior Emperor, is found with any real authority.

Since the Emperor was the representative of God, he naturally had a special relationship to the Church.[1] To begin with, from the mid-

1. See also ch. VI.

fifth century it became customary for the Emperor to be crowned by the Patriarch of Constantinople, the highest ecclesiastical authority in the Byzantine Church. Some scholars maintain that coronation came to be regarded as essential and actually conferred imperial authority. Others consider that imperial authority was independent of coronation by the Patriarch of Constantinople. The truth seems to be, as so often with Byzantine history, that the position is not static but changes. Imperial authority, though long recognised as a trust from God, was not at first regarded as being conferred by the Patriarch, though he was naturally chosen as being the appropriate person to bestow the insignia indicating that the Emperor ruled by the grace of God. It seems unlikely that the Patriarch ever acted merely 'as a layman, the first Roman citizen', as J. B. Bury thought. By the ninth century the coronation ceremony was well established. By the tenth century it was fixed in essentials and had come to be regarded as indispensable. There was only one Emperor, Constantine XI, who, for rather special reasons, was not officially crowned, and he is not always regarded as being an Emperor. Otherwise the long line of rulers from Leo I (457–474) onwards regarded it as essential that they should be crowned by the Patriarch of Constantinople, who by reason of his priesthood and his position in the ecclesiastical hierarchy performed the rite of consecrating the Emperor as vice-gerent of Christ. At the coronation of the Augusta, or a son, or daughter, the Emperor, who had been duly crowned by the Patriarch, took the crown from him and then placed it on the head of the junior. This has been taken as an argument in favour of minimising the Patriarch's part, but it was the Patriarch who in the first instance handed over the crown after the appointed prayers. Further, in the course of time, the Patriarch became responsible for vouching for the orthodoxy of the Emperor, and after the iconoclast controversy it became customary for the Emperor to sign a profession of faith before the coronation ceremony took place. This is laid down in the tenth-century book on imperial administration, and the words are given in the fourteenth-century Pseudo-Codinus' treatise *On Offices*. The statement begins with profession of belief in the creed, followed by a promise to uphold the traditions of the Church with special reference to the seven General Councils, the local synods, 'and the privileges and customs of the most holy Great Church of God' (i.e. the cathedral of Hagia Sophia, or the Holy Wisdom, in Constantinople), and it ends with mention of the Emperor's duties towards his subjects and with anathema against all heresies. Heredity, from time to time the army, or less frequently the people, gave that initial impetus which resulted in the assumption of imperial authority, but this assumption had to be signed and sealed, a trust from God, transmitted to the Emperor through the medium of the Patriarch's priesthood.

To some extent this did differentiate the Emperor from an ordinary layman. Everywhere and on all occasions his unique position, indeed his sacred position, was emphasised. He was portrayed with the nimbus. His palace was the 'sacred palace', the *domus divina* or θεῖον παλάτιον, and he himself was likened to the apostles. He had a special place in the church services; for instance at Christmas he censed the holy altar, and on Monday at the beginning of Lent he preached in the Magnaura to the court and to the people, the representatives of the demes, to inaugurate the observance of this penitential season. He entered the sanctuary with his gifts and went to the altar to receive the elements, not by intinction, but in both kinds from the Patriarch, 'as priests do'. In the acclamation at church councils he was hailed as priest-king (translated *pontifex* or *sacerdos* in the Latin *acta* of Chalcedon, and recognised as a title legitimately borne by those Emperors who were orthodox—it was refused by the Papacy to Leo the Isaurian because he was a heretic). But this appellation did not confer the priesthood on the Emperor, and he is never for instance found celebrating; it was in fact a continuation of the fiction of *privilegium* which dispensed with certain laws in favour of Julius Caesar and Octavius, and which in later days recognised the special position assigned by God to the Christian Emperor.

The very conception of a single Christian Empire implied that the Church was part of the polity and was in all respects under the general care of the Emperor, even if there were certain specific functions which he himself could not perform. The dichotomy between what was Caesar's and what was God's was not so obvious in the *imperium christianum* of East Rome as in western Christendom and it only came to the surface when the Emperor was a heretic. It was recognised that the Emperor had a special responsibility for maintaining law and order among his subjects, ecclesiastical as well as lay, and this was interpreted as including not only their conduct as individuals, but the discipline and organisation of ecclesiastical institutions (as monasteries), or ecclesiastical administration (as the re-arrangement of dioceses). The imperial novels are full of regulations of this kind. This responsibility was also exercised in the election of the greater ecclesiastics, such as the Patriarch or the bishops. When the newly elected Patriarch was consecrated, it was the Emperor who pronounced the words of institution—'this man is appointed Patriarch of Constantinople by the grace of God and by our imperial authority which proceeds from the grace of God'.

Above all, the Emperor had from the beginning a vital part in the most important organ of church government, the General Council. Constantine the Great who called the first General Council at Nicaea in 325, had said that he was 'the bishop of those outside', presumably in contrast to the assembled bishops of those organised within the Empire. In fact the Emperor had an accepted position in the councils which was not the same as that of the assembled fathers. Here again there has been misunderstanding because of the failure to realise the influence of the machinery of non-Christian times. In procedure and seating the General Council of the Church was modelled on that of the Roman senate: the council was summoned by the Emperor, the presidency belonged to the Emperor or his commissioners (corresponding to the *princeps* or consul), the Pope, or his legates, had the right of voting first (corresponding to the *princeps senatus*), and the decrees had to be signed by the Emperor. It was indeed essential to have the co-operation of the Emperor who had the authority to ensure that the canons were put into effect. Frescoes, mosaics and manuscript illustrations bear this out (and show a similar presidency being exercised over local synods by Bulgarian or Serbian rulers). How far the Emperor could influence the course of the discussion, or even impose his own views on the assembly, depended on circumstances and personality. His presence and interest were however accepted as normal, as the recorded proceedings testify. It became recognised that the Emperor could not impose his own will on the Church in matters of doctrine. On the whole it was acknowledged that one of his first duties was to uphold orthodoxy. He might take personal action in the extermination of heresy, as Alexius Comnenus did against the Bogomils in the late eleventh century, or he could summon oecumenical or local synods to deal with specific problems.

Though generally accepted, the normality of the imperial concern for the Church in all aspects of its life did not go unchallenged. But protests were rare, at least in the East Roman Empire. Churchmen such as Ambrose in the late fourth century maintained that the Emperor was within the Church not above it, and severely criticised imperial concern for dogma, and there is always present the conception, perhaps going back to Jewish times, of the Church as a higher sphere than the State and not part of it (an Augustinian as against an Eusebian view). 'The Empire,' said Pope Gelasius I in 489, 'is the son of the Church, not its ruler', and he elaborated the view of the two spheres in which the spiritual was the higher, though the Emperor was admittedly the *defensor orthodoxae*. Medieval political development in Greek and Latin Christendom took different roads, and this is to some extent reflected in their respective views on Church and State. In the East, after a period of readjustment, certain limitations on imperial control of the Church were accepted, but never to the same extent as in the West. It is unlikely that many East Romans would have wished to admit as a working principle the early ninth-century Theodore the Studite's passionate reproach, 'Emperor, do not destroy the independence of the Church. You are concerned with politics and war, that is your proper business, so leave the affairs of the Church to clergy and monks.' The truth was that both laymen and ecclesiastics were interested in theology. Thus the Emperor not only continued to legislate for the Church in disciplinary matters, but very often he also took an interest in theological problems, such as the fourteenth-century hesychast controversy, which was in part a discussion about the nature of God and how He manifested Himself. The relation of the Emperor to the Patriarch, of secular to ecclesiastical affairs in Byzantium is best expressed not by the misleading word 'caesaropapism' but as a state of 'interdependence'. Byzantium had always recognised the common interests of Church and State. Even a Justinian, autocratic as he was, could preface his sixth *Novel* with the words 'The greatest gifts which God in His love of mankind (*philanthropia*) has given from above to men are the priesthood and the Empire, the one ministering to things divine, the other guiding and taking thought for human affairs.' This was elaborated in a late ninth-century legal handbook, the *Epanogoge*,[1] in which Emperor and Patriarch are compared to soul and body, each vital to the other, each part of the same organic unity. The tenth-century John Tzimisces and others held similar views. Dissident voices, such as that of the Patriarch Michael Cerularius in the eleventh century, were overruled and not allowed to disturb the traditional relationship of Church and State. When in the fourteenth century the Emperor Andronicus II rejected Calecas' advice, the latter retorted, 'I am surprised at your commanding me to mind the business of the Church and allow you to rule the Empire at your will. For it is as if the body were to say to the soul "I do not need your companionship and will not bear your judgment and order of my actions; I will go my way, you go yours." '

Nevertheless there were changes of emphasis, and on the whole the Church steadily grew in strength after the iconoclast controversy. Medieval imperial art reflects this change. The Emperor in

1. See above, p. 40.

the post-iconoclast period appears not as in the sixth-century San Vitale as Melchisedech priest and king, but stands side by side with the Patriarch, the two symbolised as Moses and Aaron. After centuries of struggle the major doctrinal problems had been settled, and the separatist heretical provinces of the East had been lost to Islam. From the ninth century onwards what is stressed in imperial art, and reflected in literature, is not so much the Emperor in triumph as the Emperor before God, who cares above all for the preservation of orthodoxy, right belief.

As the vicegerent of Christ, the Emperor was the source of all authority. He was autocratic in the sense that there was no effective constitutional machinery whereby his actions could be regularly questioned and an alternative policy put into practice. Neither the ancient Greek city state nor the later medieval western systems found any counterpart in Byzantium. But autocracy and tyranny were by no means synonymous, and the Byzantine ruler was mindful of the traditional responsibilities of his imperial office. In practice imperial wishes generally prevailed, but there were clearly limits beyond which an Emperor could only go at his peril. It is worth remembering that not only was the Emperor bound by his coronation oath, but he, like the least of his subjects, could be excommunicated for grave sin. It is significant that a powerful Emperor, such as John Tzimisces, thought it essential to heed the patriarchal threat and amend his policy accordingly. And even in the hour of mortal danger the Emperor could not persuade his Church and people to accept ecclesiastical reunion with Rome.

Byzantine rulers accepted the principles of Roman law which they had inherited. The Emperor was the embodiment of law, the animate and living law, as he was called. The method of settling disputes and protecting the individual in society by peaceful and not violent means was in itself a limitation on unfettered autocracy. As the guardians of society within a civilised framework, Byzantine Emperors sponsored commissions to see that the legal codes were freed of accretions or impurities in the text and were not over-complicated by an accumulation of (often contradictory) interpretations of the original passages. They also introduced such alterations or additions as might be occasioned by the varying needs of the Empire. Such work is seen not only in the famous *Corpus* of Justinian, but in the codes of the eighth-, late ninth- and early tenth-century Emperors, which were supplemented by various unofficial codes and minor handbooks, such as the *Farmer's Law* probably of the late seventh century, or the *Book of the Prefect* which regulated the guilds of Constantinople in the early tenth century, as well as by the ecclesiastical rulings of the canonists. The early tenth-century work called the *Basilica* eventually became the final form of the official legal corpus. It was in Greek, the current language of the Empire, and was sponsored by Basil I and Leo VI, and it was constantly used and glossed by succeeding generations.

Side by side with this highly valued legal corpus were the courts in which the law was administered. Final appeal lay with the Emperor in his imperial court, and jurisdiction over the highest officials was reserved to him. Ordinarily cases would be heard in the local courts, either lay or ecclesiastical according to the person and cause. From the earliest recognition of Christianity the Emperor had been concerned to recognise and define the competence of both. The ecclesiastical courts would normally deal with cases in which the accused was a cleric, and had competence in civil causes if both parties were clerics. Certain cases, such as those concerning marriage, were also reserved to it. The growing power of the Church is reflected in the increasing share which it took in jurisdiction. After 1261 the demarcation between civil and ecclesiastical courts became less clear, and the imperial authority made great use of churchmen. For instance, both clerics and laymen were sent out on eyre in the later middle ages, and eventually local courts of appeal were set up in the different centres of the truncated Empire to save the expense and delay of bringing a case to the capital.

The Autocrator was responsible for the initiation of policy and the direction of the administration. He could appoint and dismiss at will. The actual office was conferred by imperial edict, but the imperial derivation of authority was symbolised by the bestowal, often at Easter, of the ceremonial clothes, together with an honorary title indicating the place which the recipient would have in court ceremonies. Such titles of rank would be conferred by the Emperor in person; the title of *magister*, for instance, would carry with it a gold-embroidered cloak, a tunic woven of white and gold thread, and a jewelled belt. Ceremonies of this kind helped to emphasise the dependence of the high officials on the Emperor, who, indeed, also paid them their salaries on Passion Sunday, as the tenth-century Italian ambassador Liutprand of Cremona noted.

The senate as an active body had ceased to be a factor of importance in the government: on occasion it showed that it could take the initiative, as at the time of Leo VI's death in 912 and during the early years of his son Constantine VII's minority, but that was unusual. Generally speaking the senate was composed of men distinguished by some title of honour and not by any real office. The Emperor's advisory circle was informal, a small group of men who owed their position to imperial choice and who were superseded at imperial will. Some measure of continuity was assured in the lower branches of the civil service and in the law courts. The machinery of tax-collection continued from day to day (as all knew), though changes in method might be introduced with imperial approval or as an imperial expedient. Inroads into the authority and resources of the central government were made by the granting of immunities (*exkousseiai*) to both lay and ecclesiastical landlords. This took various forms. The landlord might himself be responsible for collecting the taxes due from his tenants, sending them direct to the central state treasury and thus avoiding the unwelcome presence of tax collectors on his estate. Or he might be granted immunity from all or some of the taxes due, and sometimes he also had jurisdiction over his tenants. From the late eleventh century onwards grants of property in *pronoia* further weakened the imperial administration.[1]

The Byzantine civil service was a highly complex organisation and, contrary to popular belief, it was on the whole both efficient and flexible. The machinery of administration was subject to constant imperial scrutiny and it underwent considerable change during the long course of Byzantine history. It was centred in Constantinople where the highest civil officials would receive their orders from the Emperor. Some, as the Prefect of the capital, had an exalted position and clearly defined duties. Some had positions directly connected with the imperial household; such was the Grand Chamberlain who by reason of his proximity to the imperial person had great responsibility and often great influence. There were the usual civil offices as the chancery and the exchequer, each with its numerous departments. For instance there was a special financial department which dealt with supplying equipment for the army and therefore had control over the state factories. Another department was responsible for supplying horses in time of war, and its head supervised the stud-farms of Asia Minor.

By the tenth century the civil administration differed considerably in detail from that of the early fourth. Generally speaking the changes were in the direction of multiplication of the more important offices. Thus there was increasing differentiation of function with increasing dependence on the Emperor. Central control became much stricter and the great officials less independent. The decentralisation which had characterised the days of the Pretorian Prefects

1. See also p. 56.

had vanished, though there still remained the threat of over-powerful generals or wealthy land-owning magnates.

Similarly, changes were introduced in the organisation of the provinces. Military needs bred the reforms initiated by the house of Heraclius in the seventh century and continued by its successors.[1] The territorial grouping of the provinces was altered, and the new units, the themes, were placed under the control of a governor, usually called a general (*strategos*), who had supreme military and civil authority. These themes were continually being subdivided, and also added to, as fresh land was conquered, or control over lost provinces re-established, under the outstanding generals of the middle Byzantine period.[2] After the break-up of the Empire in 1204, there were still further changes, and indeed territory passed from hand to hand with such frequency that provincial administrative arrangements tended to be only a paper organisation. Nevertheless a certain core of administrative machinery was preserved, and it was largely this which enabled the Palaeologi to maintain their rule for nearly two hundred and fifty years after the Latin dismemberment of the Empire. The bureaucracy with its common language Greek thus played a considerable part in holding together the heterogeneous elements of Byzantium, both in the days when its prestige stood high and when its fortunes were on the wane. It was this administrative machinery which made it possible both to defend and to extend the frontiers of the Empire.

External affairs were in the hands of the Emperor who was the foreign minister *par excellence*. This is admirably demonstrated by the *De Administrando Imperio* which laid down the guiding principles in foreign affairs. It was drawn up in the mid-tenth century and was to be a confidential handbook for the Emperor Constantine VII's son, and would no doubt also be used by the senior officials in the foreign office. It was evidently not for general consumption, and very few copies of the manuscript appear to have been made. Imperial inclination and background did of course affect the emphasis of foreign policy. For instance Nicephorus Phocas from a wealthy Asia Minor family was more interested in the acquisition of fresh land on the eastern frontier than in defending the Danube: Constantine IX, an easy-going non-combatant, for the most part concentrated on pursuing his pleasant private life in Constantinople. Often the inadequacies of an indolent Emperor or of a minor were made good by an efficient co-Emperor, certainly until the end of the tenth century.

1. See ch. II.
2. See map of the Empire in the eleventh century on p. 45.

But whatever the personal views of individual Emperors, long frontiers and perpetual threats from hostile neighbours allowed the Byzantine foreign office little respite. By tradition its favourite weapon was diplomacy. This was exercised in various ways, many of which are expounded in the *De Administrando Imperio*. In Constantinople itself every opportunity was taken to impress guests and ambassadors. The beauty of its buildings, the strength of its fortifications and the wealth of its merchants and shipping, were more than equalled by the awe-inspiring magnificence of the imperial reception. There was a careful scale of costly presents for visitors, as well as honorary titles. This was reinforced by annual payments and special subsidies in order to secure alliances, or to play off one enemy against another, for instance Patzinak against Bulgar, or Bulgar against Russian. Malcontents and political refugees were welcomed at Constantinople for obvious reasons. In the period after the First Crusade marriages were arranged with increasing frequency between the Byzantine imperial family and western or Slav royal families, in contrast to the earlier days when the *De Administrando Imperio* carefully pointed out that it was normally unsuitable for those born in the purple to marry a non-Byzantine (though this did of course on occasion happen). Thus, although the main principles of Byzantine diplomacy remained unchanged, there was a certain flexibility in their application, and policy was adapted to suit the needs of changing circumstances.

The responsibility for the maintenance of an army and navy was also the sovereign's; his was the choice of the generals (or admirals) in whose hands the conduct of expeditions lay, though often, like a Basil II or a Michael IV, he might choose to lead his forces himself. An army was essential in an Empire ringed with enemies; it was as vital to the State 'as the head is to the body'. Before the eleventh century, troops were recruited as far as possible from indigenous sources, mainly from the Armenians and Isaurians who made excellent soldiers. From the seventh century onwards they were normally paid by the grant of a hereditary military holding, receiving as well an annual cash sum for each year's service up to a total of twelve years. Special imperial efforts were made to protect these soldier-farmers, but in the eleventh century it was clear that they were decreasing in number, largely because their lands were bought up by the great magnates, or disrupted by constant Turkish invasions. From the twelfth century onwards native defences took a different and more aristocratic, perhaps a more feudal, form with the increased use of grants in *pronoia*. These were generally substantial, and originally inalienable, grants to magnates in return for military service.[1] Extensive use was also made of professional soldiers, both native and foreign. This was expensive and owing to depleted resources officers sometimes had to be paid by grants giving them the right to collect imperial dues from specified districts or estates, an unpopular device since it led to the wholesale exploitation of the countryside.

Before the Empire began to break up the provincial troops were based on the themes. Special provision was made for the frontier districts, which were garrisoned, and dominated, by a series of marcher lords. Life in the eastern marches in the tenth century stands revealed in the story of Digenis Akritas, with his Christian mother and his father a convert from Islam, whose exploits and adventures appear in epic and folk ballad. In Constantinople itself, palace guards, both mounted and infantry, were stationed, as well as the imperial bodyguard. This latter contained many foreign mercenaries. In the eleventh century the Varangian bodyguard had become renowned and attracted recruits from distant countries. Originally composed of Russo-Scandinavian soldiers, it was by the late eleventh century mainly Anglo-Saxon.

Details of the army, with its cavalry and infantry, its baggage and vital equipment, mobile field artillery and engines of war, are revealed in surviving sources, particularly various military handbooks. The art of warfare was highly perfected. Special attention was given to defence; every effort was made to conserve resources by not taking the offensive, but the methods of the enemy were carefully studied in preparation for occasions when open battle was unavoidable. The excellence of its army was one of the reasons why Byzantium so long preserved its frontiers intact. Its soldiers were also sustained not only by the thought of their duty and reward in this world, but by the firm belief that they were warriors in the Christian cause against the infidel and would find their final happiness in the world to come. They were accompanied on campaign by special orators (*cantatores*) who roused them by stirring exhortations; they had with them clergy, and they began and ended their day with a service. Their battle cry was 'the Cross has conquered', and they were moved by a crusading spirit, conscious of the presence of the heavenly host, particularly the vigilant militant saints, such as St George or St Theodore, under whose special protection they fought.

1. P. Lemerle, 'Recherches sur le régime agraire à Byzance: la terre militaire à l'époque des Comnènes' in *Cahiers de Civilisation Médiévale*, 2 (1959) reconsiders this. The whole problem of the *pronoia* is still under discussion.

Side by side with this indomitable fighting force the navy took its place. It was not regarded as the senior service, but could claim its due share of the credit for averting the oncoming waves of Muslim attack. There were maritime as well as military themes in the Aegean and coastal regions of south-east and south Asia Minor, later aided by the coastal themes of Greece. Their job was to supply naval recruits and equipment. There was also an 'imperial' fleet stationed at Constantinople. These fleets played a decisive part in driving back the Arabs and preserving the capital in the seventh and eighth centuries, and in regaining some control over the Aegean in the Macedonian period. It was indeed with truth that the Emperor Nicephorus II could assert in 968 to Otto I's ambassador, the touchy Liutprand of Cremona, that he alone enjoyed maritime supremacy. The effective weapon of the Byzantine navy was the deadly Greek fire, a burning substance apparently compounded of various ingredients, such as sulphur and saltpetre, and hurled from a catapult on to the enemy ships.

Byzantine misfortune from the eleventh century onwards affected its naval, no less than its military, strength. The State lacked the material resources for its upkeep and could not compete with the growing maritime power of the Italian cities, particularly Venice and Genoa. Ships even had to be laid up and unemployed Byzantine sailors took service with the Turks or turned to piracy. But this was in the period after 1204 when Byzantium was a minor state. For at least four hundred years from Heraclius to Basil II both army and navy had proved effective instruments with which to support Byzantine diplomacy and to keep back the infidel.

VI

THE ORTHODOX CHURCH:

THE CHRISTIAN LIFE AND THE LAITY

I

The recognition of the Christian religion by Constantine the Great in the early fourth century could not affect the essentials of Christianity nor alter the nature of the divinely constituted Church. It did however initiate certain changes. The old Roman Empire with its many different religions was replaced by a Christian *imperium romanum*. In the early middle ages imperial unity was disrupted in the West, but in spite of political and linguistic differences there emerged a society retaining a measure of unity based on its common Christian faith. This was medieval Christendom, consisting at first of the young states of the Latin West and the Byzantine Empire of the Greek and oriental East Mediterranean, to which were later added the converted Slav peoples. There were also certain other Christian countries, as Armenia or Ethiopia, as well as communities living in non-Christian polities, for instance in the Persian Empire, and later in the Muslim principalities.

Even before it was allowed to worship openly and in peace the Christian Church was widespread and had its strongholds, notably Rome, Antioch and Alexandria. In the course of the fourth and fifth centuries it was organised apace, following the pattern of the secular government. It was split into provinces under metropolitans. The chief, or 'arch', metropolitans were those of Rome, Antioch and Alexandria, the old sees of apostolic foundation, of which Rome had always had primacy of honour. During this period Jerusalem and Constantinople took their place amongst these bishops of first rank. Thus there came into being the five great patriarchates, the pentarchy, into which medieval Christendom was divided. Jerusalem had special claims to veneration and to this high rank. The importance of Constantinople was derived not from apostolic foundation or special association with the struggles of the early Church but from its position as the imperial residence and the new capital. This was recognised by the General Council of Constantinople in 381 when it stated that the bishop of Constantinople was second only to the bishop of Old Rome and had the same prerogatives of honour because Constantinople was New Rome. In 451 at the end of the Council of Chalcedon, when the Roman legates were absent, this was reaffirmed at a special sitting in the so-called twenty-eighth canon of Chalcedon. Though at the time not accepted by the Papacy, this canon was regarded by the Orthodox Church as a valid statement of its rights. It was also bitterly resented by Alexandria and Antioch, but in any case Muslim conquests from the seventh century onwards were to deprive these two cities of much of their influence and Constantinople was destined to become the most important ecclesiastical centre in the Christian East, also exercising considerable influence over northern Slav territories.

From the fourth century onwards the common problems of discipline and dogma were discussed and dealt with in ecclesiastical assemblies. At the highest level there were the General Councils, the first of which was convened by Constantine the Great at Nicaea in A.D. 325. All the bishops (or their representatives if they could not come in person) were summoned, and the decisions of these synods were binding on the whole Church. Proceedings throughout were conducted under imperial auspices, and illustrated the close co-operation between Church and State. The sessions ended with acclamations for the orthodox rulers and the canons were signed by them, thus ensuring that these would receive the support of the secular authority.

The first seven of these General Councils were recognised by all patriarchates. After the ninth century there was not the same need for general assemblies; the main period of doctrinal definition had passed and problems of discipline could be dealt with on a regional basis. From the mid-eleventh century onwards there was also another obstacle in the way of fraternal conferences: this was the growing rift between the Latin West and the Byzantine Empire, particularly aggravated by the aggression of the Fourth Crusade in 1204. In the later middle ages the Church had problems of a different nature, but the essential preliminary to any General Council was whether Constantinople would make 'oecumenical' discussions possible by agreeing to ecclesiastical reunion with Rome.

The emergence of Constantinople as the capital of the medieval East Roman Empire and the loss of its rivals Antioch and Alexandria to the infidel inevitably emphasised the importance of the Patriarch of Constantinople, the head of the Byzantine Church. In the face of Rome's protests he had taken the title of 'oecumenical', though it is true that this was not in the sense of ruler over the whole Church. His authority had been increased at the expense of Rome when the Emperor Leo III in 732 transferred the provinces of South Italy, Greece and parts of the Balkans to his jurisdiction. Relations with Rome had been further strained by the papal alliance with the western rulers and the subsequent papal inauguration of a western line of Emperors in 800. The Byzantine Patriarch came into close contact with the Emperor. He received his profession of faith, crowned him, could advise and on occasion admonish. The Autocrator was the more powerful figure, often largely responsible for the Patriarch's election and capable of procuring his resignation or deposition. Nevertheless the Patriarch had his own place in the closely linked spheres of Church and State, and after 1204 it was usually the Patriarch who took the lead in resisting the Emperor's attempts to achieve reunion with Rome, and in this he was strongly supported by laity, monks and secular clergy. Apart from his priestly functions he was specially responsible for the maintenance of Christian instruction and discipline within the Church. After the settlement of the major doctrinal controversies in the General Councils, the Patriarch worked mainly through the standing synod in Constantinople (*synodos endemousa*). This had originally been made up of bishops living in the capital but from the tenth century onwards it was attended by metropolitans and autocephalous archbishops. Here problems of liturgy were settled, perhaps a new festival instituted, points of controversy dealt with, as for instance whether a particular cult could be permitted or not. Punishment was also meted out to offending churchmen, for the synod acted as a court of justice as well as a deliberative and legislative body.

Throughout the life of the medieval Orthodox Church the secular and ecclesiastical authorities worked together, the one supplementing the other, as is admirably illustrated by the nearest Byzantine equivalent to the western corpus of canon law. Its most important collection of ecclesiastical rulings was known as the 'Nomocanon in fourteen titles'. It consisted of legislation by the Emperor and by the Church, as well as other matter which was regarded as authoritative. The fourteen titles really applied originally only to the first part which gave canonical rulings on subjects ranging from orthodox faith to the administration of ecclesiastical property. It was followed by texts cited *in extenso*, as the so-called eighty-five canons of the apostles and certain patristic passages, and it concluded with the relevant secular laws. It was originally the sixth-century private collection of John Scholasticus of Antioch, who became Patriarch of Constantinople. On the basis of this work, the 'Nomocanon in fourteen titles' emerged in the seventh century and was accepted by the Council in Trullo (691) and by later councils. In the course of the middle ages it was brought up to date from time to time, and it went through four editions, the last being made by the canonist Balsamon at the end of the twelfth century.

The Patriarch was at the apex of the hierarchy of the Byzantine Church. Under him there were the metropolitans set over the ecclesiastical provinces, each of which was divided into bishoprics. Bishops not under a metropolitan were called autocephalous archbishops. Metropolitans were at first chosen by the Patriarch from three nominees, later by the standing synod in Constantinople. Bishops were chosen by the metropolitan from three names put forward by the provincial synod, and the imperial claim to confirm the election was resisted. The Emperors did however retain their right to promote or demote by altering the status of a high cleric; thus a bishop might be created metropolitan or autocephalous bishop, often without regard to the practical consequences. The metropolitan had rights of general supervision over his province, but though he could punish offending bishops he had to be careful not to infringe their rights in their own dioceses. Bishops had to be thirty-five years old and men of some education who knew the Psalter by heart, and if married they had to separate from their wives. Latterly it became usual for bishops to be monks, as also in the case of the Patriarch, in contrast to the days when a distinguished layman and humanist such as Photius could be elected. Within his diocese the bishop was responsible for all ecclesiastical matters, such as the discipline of his clergy or of the monasteries, as also for the spiritual well-being and instruction of the laity. He had certain rights of jurisdiction when clerics were involved and he might be called in to arbitrate by the laity.

In his cathedral church the bishop was assisted by clergy of various ranks, the more important of whom filled special offices connected either with the work of the cathedral or with diocesan administration. Similar arrangements, though on a more elaborate scale, were found in the metropolitan churches. Hagia Sophia in Constantinople, 'the Great Church' as it was called, had an enormous staff, limited

D

from time to time by patriarchal and imperial efforts. In 612 the Patriarch, with imperial support, reduced the number of its clergy to eighty priests, one-hundred-and-fifty deacons, forty deaconesses, seventy sub-deacons, one-hundred-and-sixty readers, twenty-five cantors and seventy-five doorkeepers; and this was in addition to a certain number of permitted 'extras'. In the Great Church the leading figure after the Patriarch was the *syncellus*. He was the *familiaris* and confidant of the Patriarch, his spiritual father, as also that of the Emperor. There also developed a group of leading officials who shared between them the work connected not only with Hagia Sophia itself but with the patriarchal administration in general. For instance the Great Chartophylax (the keeper of documents) began by taking charge of the patriarchal archives. He became a kind of librarian, secretary, and chancellor rolled into one, for his work expanded to include supervision of clergy, ordinations, episcopal elections, and indeed complete control of the patriarchal chancery. His importance is shown by his place at pontifical mass when he stood near the holy door and at the moment of communion summoned the clergy with the words, 'Priests and deacons, come and receive your King and God.' This group of major officials found its counterpart in the curias of metropolitans and bishops throughout the Orthodox Church. They are the eastern equivalent of the four chief dignitaries (*quattuor personae*) of the medieval English cathedral chapter. Ecclesiastical organisation bore a certain similarity at different levels and in different parts of Christendom.

In the Orthodox Church the great majority of the secular clergy, that is, the orders below that of bishop, were allowed to be married, provided this had taken place before they were ordained sub-deacon. They evidently engaged in all kinds of trade until prohibited by canon law. It would of course be unfair to deduce from conciliar rulings that the majority of clergy regularly attended cabaret shows or ran betting establishments. But their status was often a low one, and many did agricultural work in the fields like the present-day *papas* in the Greek countryside. When property was sold they went with the estate like the *paroikoi*, or dependent tenants, in the village. These lower clergy might serve in two different kinds of church: the 'general' or parish church (the *catholicon*), i.e. the church under the diocesan bishop who nominated its incumbent; and the chapel belonging perhaps to a monastery, perhaps to a private person or even group of individuals who had clubbed together to found it. Sometimes the villagers would assist the little nucleus of a new community in building the monastic chapel, as was the experience of the eleventh-century St Dorotheus in Asia Minor. It is evident from various lives of the saints and other sources that the needs of the countryside as well as the towns were mostly provided for by monastic or private foundations which far outnumbered the 'catholic' churches.

The Church was not poor, and imperial legislation abounded in regulations controlling the administration of its property. Patriarchal administration was in the hands of the Great Oeconomus. Within the diocese the bishop might appoint an oeconomus as steward of property belonging to particular churches or institutions, or it might be controlled by the clergy in charge. Landed property was sometimes granted out on lease, though in practice it was often found that the church lost by this. Church property could not normally be alienated, not even for imperial needs. Sometimes Emperors made laymen the guardians of a monastic foundation, thereby allowing them to take charge of the house's property, provided that they allowed the monks sufficient for their livelihood—a system that readily lent itself to abuse.

In addition to donations and legacies from the faithful, the bishop received a tax, the *canonicon*, which was defined and made compulsory in the eleventh century. The villagers paid partly in money, partly in kind, according to the number of families in the village; priests paid him one gold coin (*nomisma*) a year, and monasteries also had to pay, unless they sent this direct to the Patriarch because they had been founded by him and were under his direct control.[1] Certain other dues were paid on special occasions, as marriage fees. Dues were also paid on the occasion of an ordination, but not for the ordination. Such gifts were regulated by custom and imperial decree. Simony was strictly condemned (even the eleventh-century anti-Greek Cardinal Humbert found something to praise in the Orthodox Church on this account). From his revenue the bishop would normally provide for his cathedral clergy, unlike the western system of separate prebends. He was also responsible for churches which had no endowment. In the later middle ages these *catholica* or parish churches were sometimes provided for by revenue from a special grant of church property (*klerikaton*) which was leased to the incumbent.

---

1. Such monasteries were called 'stauropegial'; see pp. 113 n. 5, 115.

II

Within this framework the Orthodox Church lived its everyday life, preserving its tradition unbroken to the present day. Almost from the beginning the Church had shown itself to be the heir of Graeco-Roman, as well as of East Mediterranean, traditions: it therefore defined its terms and articulated Christian belief, often in an atmosphere of bitter and prolonged controversy. Thus in the days of the early Church and of the early Byzantine Empire the theological foundations of Christianity were laid. By the ninth century the worst dangers—mainly disputes about the nature of the Trinity and of Christ—had been overcome; 'the Church of the seven General Councils' had emerged, firmly convinced of its sacred mission to preserve and to spread the true faith. In common with the rest of Christendom the theological heritage of the Orthodox Church was enshrined in the patristic writings and the canons of the oecumenical councils which interpreted the Scriptures and the liturgical tradition of the Church. The works of the Greek fathers, particularly of the fourth century, constantly shone out as a beacon to guide troubled churchmen through four centuries and more of perplexity and challenge. By the time that the iconoclast controversy was beginning to die down in the ninth century, orthodox teaching had been summed up, restated as it were, by the last of the Greek fathers, John of Damascus, in his *Fount of Knowledge*. This culminated with an exposition of doctrine known as the *De fide orthodoxa*, which was used in a Latin translation in the West from the twelfth century onwards. It is often assumed of the Orthodox Church, as of the Byzantine Empire, that it 'preserved' rather than developed. Far from it. Tradition, to be maintained, must develop as it is handed from generation to generation. Byzantium was a Christian Empire in the fullest sense: its passionate interest in theological discussion did not suddenly cease with the restoration of icon veneration and the absence of major theological controversy within its gates. At no period can it be said that Christianity was not a living issue, and Byzantine concern for it was accompanied by a full range of literary activity. The implications of orthodoxy left ample scope for discussion and development, as well as for controversy. Churchmen and laity alike applied their humanist outlook and classical background to the elucidation of the Scriptures and patristic writings. Commentaries, and treatises on particular points, homilies of every kind were poured out by each generation. Byzantine theological interests varied. In the eleventh century under Symeon the New Theologian there was a marked development of that form of spirituality which was to come to its full flowering in the hesychast movement in the fourteenth century. Hesychasm raised a major theological controversy. The views of anti-hesychast and pro-hesychast are put forward respectively in the histories of Nicephoras Gregoras and John Cantacuzenus, and these one-time friends became so estranged that they could not even bear to speak to each other. There were many conflicting currents and it is sometimes difficult to disentangle theological and political partisanship, but the movement, though open to misunderstanding, was in reality an integral part of orthodox spirituality. This fruitful development was closely connected with Mt Athos and is indicative of the extent to which the living wood of Byzantium was now to be found in its Church and not in its political institutions.

There was another aspect to the theological vigilance of the Orthodox Church. The Christian tradition in all its fullness was to be enjoyed by the faithful, but in order to ensure this, it was necessary to keep watch lest heresy crept in. The Byzantine, like the Western, Church had to deal both with individuals who had been led astray, often inadvertently, and with popular movements which were far more difficult to eradicate, being widespread and due to a variety of causes. The Church certainly did not forbid the use of pagan authors, but it assumed that these would be read with discrimination. It was easy for an adventurous or sceptical mind to overstep the bounds and find it was propounding views not in accordance with Christian teaching. Photius in an impish moment is even said to have put forward unorthodox statements to see if he could catch out a Patriarch who affected to do without intellectual weapons. Others, as Michael Psellus in the mid-eleventh century, at once retrieved a false step by a swift profession of orthodoxy. John Italus, an ardent student of Plato and Aristotle, who followed Psellus as professor of philosophy in the university of Constantinople, was not so adroit. The story of his condemnation for heretical views and his public recantation from the pulpit of Hagia Sophia is related by Anna Comnena with somewhat smug satisfaction as yet another illustration of her father's care for orthodoxy. Italus' errors are anathematised in the *Synodicon* (a list of heresies to be abjured) which is read in Lent on Orthodoxy Sunday. He came to grief, it was held, because he failed to realise that classical literature provided intellectual discipline but not the Christian truth. To the end of its days Byzantium had trouble with its intellectuals, down to Gemisthus Plethon who reverted to out and out Platonism.

A more subtle danger lurked in the widespread heresy which threatened to undermine the whole position of the Church in certain areas. This movement was dualist in character, and perhaps originated in Asia Minor, long the home of such heretics as the Paulicians. In the tenth century a form of this dualist heresy developed in the Balkans. It took its name from its leader, the *pop* (i.e. priest) Bogomil. At this time Bulgaria was in process of being absorbed into the Byzantine Empire and when its conquest was finally achieved under Basil II in the early eleventh century the insidious heresy crept into the very stronghold of orthodoxy. It was doubly dangerous in that it was not only an attack on Christian doctrine and the organisation of the Christian Church but had social and economic and political implications. In Bulgaria at any rate it was allied to anti-Byzantine feeling, and in addition was directed against the wealth of both lay and ecclesiastical landowners. The heresy was vigorously combated, particularly by the Comnenian Emperors working in close co-operation with the Church. But it was never entirely quenched in the Balkans. The Bogomils lingered on until the Turkish conquest and after, and their fantastically grotesque tombs may still be seen in Bosnia. The heresy is said to have affected Mt Athos itself in the fourteenth century, but this charge may have been part of the anti-hesychast propaganda against the Holy Mountain.

In addition to watching over the religious life of their own household, Orthodox churchmen were aware of their responsibilities towards those of other creeds. Euthymius Zigabenus, at the request of the Emperor Alexius Comnenus, wrote a handbook exposing the religious errors of the major heresies, including the Jews and the Muslims. John of Damascus had regarded Mohammedanism as a Christian heresy; he was well-equipped to write a treatise against it, for he knew Arabic and in his refutation could use the Koran at first hand. Polemic against every form of heresy was in the competent hands of theologians, both lay and ecclesiastical, and was continually being turned out until the last days of the Empire. Other, and perhaps more fruitful, steps were also taken, in personal discussions which took place between bishops and rabbis, between Muslim and Christian, or between Armenian and Orthodox. As far as Islam went the honours were divided, for either side had its converts. In fact when Archbishop Gregory Palamas was captured by the Ottomans in the mid-fourteenth century and took part in disputation with Muslims, he learnt that Islam was particularly proud of the numbers converted to its faith in Asia Minor. The really constructive missionary work of the Orthodox Church was done in its early days amongst its pagan neighbours, or further afield, when countless churchmen toiled to convert Slav or Khazar. Some, like Cyril and Methodius, still enjoy a world-wide reputation for their work; but most remain anonymous, or, like the eleventh-century John of Euchaita's uncle who worked in the Balkans, are only known by chance reference buried in a sermon or funeral oration. In missionary work of this kind the Church had a comparatively virgin field, very different from the situation when rival creeds had already hardened in a framework of an older civilisation, or were perhaps a heretical offshoot of the Christian body itself, as the Nestorian and Monophysite churches.

The Orthodox Church took care to maintain its vigilance within the Empire and lost no opportunity of promoting its cause by public disputation or by published propaganda, and indeed by wars against the infidel, yet this did not preclude diplomatic relations or even the recognition of a rival way of life, particularly with eastern powers. Constantinople could regard Persia or the Saracens as powers which it could respect. An early tenth-century Patriarch of Constantinople even wrote to a Muslim ruler, 'As the two great luminaries of heaven outshine all others, so do the Saracens and the Romans, and so we should therefore live in friendship, in spite of our different ways of life and worship.'[1] This may have the ring of diplomacy about it and sentiments of this kind did not prevent the outbreak of frequent wars; but arrangements were usually permitted which allowed visitors or merchants or mercenaries of another creed or rite their own place of worship. Thus the Latins had their own churches, in particular the Venetians and Genoese, who became numerous from the twelfth century onwards and acquired their own quarters in the City or across the Golden Horn. Even the distant English (of whom a number served in the imperial bodyguard) could find something peculiarly their own in the church founded in Constantinople by a rich fellow-countryman at the end of the eleventh century, where lamps burnt at night before the icons of its two patron saints, St Nicholas and St Augustine of Canterbury.

Thus in practice there was a measure of toleration which official relations and the official attitude often conceal. There is a profundity and a warmth of feeling in the remark made by the two patricians from the capital in the story which tells of the finding of the Virgin's robe and its translation to Constantinople. For generations it had been handed down from virgin to virgin within a certain Jewish family. The travellers reached this Jewess's home in a little

1. Migne, *Patrologia Graeca*, vol. CXI, col. 28B.

village in Galilee, and that night besought her to tell them the real reason for the divine power which dwelt in the house, saying, 'For our God and your God is one and the same God.'[1] Words of this kind are a reminder that the Byzantines were not bigoted. Indeed a measure of toleration was often taken for granted and in no way lessened their devotion to orthodoxy.

III

The farmer or townsman, housewife or child, would not normally be engaged in polemic or with doctrinal developments, though the maintenance of right doctrine concerned them as much as it did theologians or statesmen. Like monks and clergy, laity, whether scholars or craftsmen, were part of the body of the faithful, and it was the supreme concern of the Church to care for their spiritual life. Their special needs were provided for within the diocesan framework. Often monasteries and hermits supplemented the work of the secular clergy, but their activities were not part of the normal diocesan provision for parishioners. The laity, no less than the newly converted, had to be instructed. From childhood upwards they were taught by their priests and by their bishop. It is clear from synodal rulings and other evidence that the clergy taught the Scriptures and otherwise educated young children, and if they were very troublesome they might give them a beating if they wished. It was the special responsibility of the bishop to preach both to his clergy and to the people. The Council in Trullo in 691 laid down that this was expected every Sunday, and if possible on weekdays as well. This obligation was evidently taken very seriously. The Byzantines were most prolific sermon writers. Many of their homilies have survived. In them, 'the shepherd and pastor' of his flock would explain the meaning of various parts of the Bible, often expounding the patristic interpretation of a particular passage, or speaking of the liturgy and the other sacraments, or the special significance of a patronal festival. This duty was shared by all from the humblest parish priest to the Patriarch. And the Emperors themselves wrote sermons and delivered them before high ecclesiastics and imperial officials on special occasions, as at the beginning of Lent.

Profound understanding of the faith and a deep devotional life are reflected in many sermons, as well as in mystical writings. How far experience of this kind came to most men and women remains unknown. But all were bound together in a living fellowship by the

1. See N. H. Baynes, *Byzantine Studies*, p. 247.

sacraments. The Orthodox Christian was baptised into the Church, confirmed by the sacrament of the Holy Spirit and, when need be, purified by penance. He could understand in some measure the fullest meaning of the Christian life when he took part in the central act of public worship, the eucharist, or, as the Byzantines usually called it, 'the divine liturgy'. Art and theology, music and poetry, were integrated in the celebration of the liturgy. Byzantine artists expressed their awareness of the supernatural world by so representing Christ and the celestial hierarchy in mosaic or fresco on the dome and walls of their churches that the heavenly host seemed present with the faithful in the body of the building below. Byzantine music was closely linked to the words of the liturgy. As this service was enriched by the addition of canticles and hymns, so its music was developed. Liturgical poetry and its tunes grew more elaborate.[1] They were often antiphonally divided between precentor and people and were interwoven between the lessons and psalms of the office or the different parts of the liturgy.

The version of the liturgy used in the Greek Church was that of Constantinople, i.e. it was based on the liturgy of St Basil and of St John Chrysostom. The liturgy began with that of the Catechumens, when the 'Little Entrance' was made with the singing of the 'Thrice-Holy', followed by the lessons and the sermon. Then came the liturgy of the Faithful, with prayers and the 'Great Entrance', the creed and the commemoration of the living and the dead. After this was the central act of the Holy Sacrifice. It is clear that the liturgy was celebrated frequently. Balsamon wrote that those trying to lead a pure life might communicate daily, whether cleric or layman, though this was not the normal rule.

The Church permeated the life of the people. Its blessing was sought on every form of activity. There were special rituals for blessing the fishing fleet or the harvest, cattle or houses, just as cities and shrines had their own special protectors among the saints, from the Mother of God, the patron of the City, to the humbler guardian angel to whom John of Euchaita dedicated one of his poems. This desire, like the Byzantine reverence for the ascete, the holy man, was rooted in a belief in the power of intercession and a sense of the close ties between the seen and unseen worlds. Thus the more lowly aspects of human life were sanctified to their right use. Likewise the laity, no less than the monk or cleric, might enjoy the full member-

1. Recent research has succeeded in deciphering the different forms of medieval Byzantine notation. Versions of the living tradition may be heard in Greece, or closer at hand in the monastery of Grottaferrata near Rome.

D*

ship of the Church which was the mystical body of Christ. One of
the best expositions of the meaning of this is found in the fourteenth-
century Nicholas Cabasilas' *On Life in Christ*. As he says, it is not
necessary to go into the desert to find this life, for it is implanted in
every Christian by baptism and is fed by the other sacraments,
particularly the divine liturgy.

VII

THE MONASTIC WORLD:
THE RELIGIOUS VOCATION

Christian monasticism first grew up in Egypt in the late third and early fourth centuries. It was a way of life voluntarily adopted by those who wished to follow more closely the gospel precepts and to master their passions and evil desires so that they would become sufficiently perfect to have some knowledge of God in this world and hereafter to enjoy Him for ever. Asceticism as such had long been known, but from the early fourth century onwards monasticism was a special development of this within the framework of the Christian Church. One of its distinguishing features was the withdrawal of the individual from ordinary everyday life in family surroundings. Warfare against the many demons who tempted the Christian in his daily path was carried out either in solitude or within a group of men pledged to observe a special discipline.

The first monks were St Antony and the other desert fathers of Egypt who left their homes and went to live in the solitude of the desert. They attracted considerable publicity and so many followers that their 'solitude' was not always exactly what they had envisaged and desired. The movement in Egypt crystallised into two main streams, the eremitic and the cenobitic. St Antony's example of hermit life was widely copied, though it is essential to remember that hermits did not always live in entire isolation. Often they had disciples grouped round them; the beginner usually started by attaching himself to a proved ascete who acted as his spiritual father. A frequent modification of the solitary way of life was the lavra,[1] or group of individual hermit dwellings in the vicinity of a more

1. From the Greek *laura*, an alley or marketway; see D. J. Chitty, *The Desert a City*, p. 15.

experienced monk; these ascetes would gather together on certain occasions, as for instance services on Saturday and Sunday. This was a halfway house between the entirely solitary anchorite and the monk who lived the 'common' life.

The *coenobium*,[1] or monastery *par excellence* in the western sense, grew up in Egypt at the same time as the eremitic life. Its founder was an Egyptian, the pagan soldier Pachomius who became converted to Christianity. After a trial run as a hermit, Pachomius realised that this made demands beyond the powers of most, and he organised corporate ascetic life at Tabennisi on the Nile in the early fourth century. So rapidly did the movement grow that when Pachomius died he had under him a congregation of eleven houses (two of which were for women). Pachomius was the head of his community, as well as the general superior over the whole group of houses. The main essentials of daily life stand out: prayer and services in common, private meditation and devotions, the bare minimum in the way of meals (usually eaten together in the refectory), manual labour and the performance of necessary domestic and administrative duties. Within this framework there were variations, both now in the experimental period and later. In fourth-century Egypt the fully developed liturgical Hours (the daily round of monastic services) were as yet unknown and communion was celebrated on Saturdays and Sundays. But already in this primitive monasticism the precepts of spiritual life and the rules of external conduct which distinguished later monastic movements in the Orthodox Church were discernible. Again and again the spirituality of both eastern and western monasticism looks back to the writings of the Egyptian fathers, such as the *Sayings of the Fathers (Apophthegmata Patrum)* or the *Life of St Antony*, that pattern for the later lives of the saints.

The essential characteristic of cenobitic life was to be the daily performance of the Office and Divine Liturgy by a community owing unswerving obedience to their superior. By the end of the fourth century this had been established throughout the Christian world, especially in the East Mediterranean. Hermit cells, lavras, and cenobitic houses were filled with men aspiring to serve God in this way. Both monasticism and the Church were particularly indebted to the fourth-century church father St Basil the Great, bishop of Caesarea in Asia Minor, whose support of the new monastic movement gave it discipline and direction. Basil, unlike Pachomius or Antony, was a learned man capable of clearly articulating his

1. Literally 'common life' (*koinos bios*).

views on monasticism, though he left no rule comparable to that of the western St Benedict of Nursia. His so-called 'Rule' is a series of answers to questions arising out of the problems of monastic life. His best known statement in this respect is probably that in which he said that the cenobitic life is superior to that of the solitary, because he considered that only in company with his fellow beings could a man fulfil the divine commandment to love his neighbour as himself.[1] It is possible that his emphasis has been exaggerated by later writers. St Basil's friend St Gregory of Nazianzus wrote about him that he most admirably reconciled and united the solitary and the common life and founded cells for ascetics and hermits near the cenobitic communities.[2] However, whatever St Basil may, or may not, have intended to imply, it is a fact that eremitic and lavra life continued to flourish in the East Roman Empire side by side with, and sometimes as part of, cenobitic establishments.

The development of all kinds of monasticism was marked in Palestine and Syria. Here the new movement rooted early and rapidly expanded until checked by the Arab invasions of the seventh century. Palestine was particularly favoured soil because of its intimate association with the earthly life of Christ. Now with the growth of cells, lavras and houses it offered an added attraction to the pilgrim in its holy monks who could give special blessings and spiritual advice by reason of their sanctity. There were both *coenobia* and anchorites, but the lavra predominated. Though allowing the individual greater responsibility for self-discipline within certain limits, the lavra, like the cenobitic house, had its rules, including obedience to the superior. Like the Egyptian monks, those of Palestine left a corpus of writings which reveal the exuberant variety of their monasticism, as well as the progress already made in working out the appropriate discipline for the different establishments and for the individual. Monastic vigour permeates the lively works of various sixth- and early seventh-century writers, as the lives by Cyril of Scythopolis or the varied jottings on the spiritual life (*Pratum Spirituale*) by John Moschus, or the *Ladder of Paradise* (*Scala Paradisi*) of John Climacus. These Greek works were translated into Slavonic, thus transmitting this tradition to the Balkans and Russia. They were also used in Orthodox monastic circles after Palestine had been lost to the Empire.

The real core of the medieval Byzantine Empire was Asia Minor,

1. *Longer Rule*, 7. That it is necessary with a view to pleasing God to live with like-minded persons, and that solitude is difficult and dangerous.
2. Greg. Naz. *Or.*, 43, 62 (On Basil).

Greece and the islands, with parts of the Balkans, and here, too, no district was without its monks. Byzantium also exercised considerable influence over monastic settlements in Sicily and South Italy until the end of the eleventh century and the establishment of the Normans. The outstanding monastic leader of the middle Byzantine period was St Theodore the Studite. True to Byzantine feeling for tradition, he drew freely on the past, particularly on the ascetic writings of St Basil of Caesarea which he read and re-read. He even said that Christ spoke through St Basil. Born in the mid-eighth century, Theodore lived and suffered at the time of the iconoclast controversy. He entered a monastery in Bithynia in Asia Minor and later moved to the Studite house in Constantinople where he became abbot in the early ninth century. Theodore and his house staunchly defended the traditional veneration of icons. More important here is his work as a spiritual director and a monastic reformer. He has left a number of addresses to his monks and sermons which reveal him as an inspired guide in the quest for the *visio Dei*. His testament and letters, and indeed his ascetical teaching, show his concern for the discipline of monastic life and the right ordering of the services and the mastery of liturgical intricacies. Theodore, like Basil, advocated moderation in the practice of asceticism, but he also emphasised absolute obedience in the common life, stressing the responsibilities of the abbot both in administration and in spiritual direction. Under Theodore's supervision the Studite house in the south-west corner of Constantinople became one of the first monasteries of the Empire, powerful and wealthy, the house to which boys of the imperial family could be sent for their upbringing, or which could offer guidance to the younger foundations in Kievan Russia.

By the mid-ninth century when Theodore the Studite died the accepted principles of Byzantine cenobitic life had been defined. It sometimes seems to puzzle western historians that they cannot find in the Eastern Church those 'orders' which characterise Latin monasticism. In the Orthodox world there was however both elasticity and a regulated norm, though enthusiasm for the monastic life was never marshalled with such feeling for legal definition as in the West. Examination of conciliar rulings, imperial laws, the foundation charters of individual houses, the comments of canonists, as well as the literary sources, particularly the lives of the saints, reveals in the East variety of cenobitic foundation as well as a wealth of spiritual experience, both eremitic and otherwise, on much of which the Latin and Slav worlds drew, both through translation and through personal knowledge.

From its inception monasticism, brought within the ecclesiastical framework by the wisdom of such church leaders as St Athanasius or St Basil, had been regulated as need arose by means of decrees in general and local councils, by imperial legislation and by patriarchal rulings. This was essential both to preserve diocesan authority and to harness this vast reservoir of energy, this spiritual powerhouse, to the needs of the Church. During the heated debates over heresies, particularly from the fourth to the seventh centuries, the monks had shown that they could be unpleasantly powerful hangers-on at councils, as well as influential centres of resistance in their own territory. Many of the disciplinary decrees of the early councils attempted to remove such abuses. Canon 4 of the Council of Chalcedon (451) plainly stated the problem and proposed a remedy.

'Those who lead a true and genuine monastic life should be given the honour which is their due. There are some however who make the monastic state an excuse for causing trouble in the churches and in political affairs, and they wander aimlessly around the cities and even undertake to set up monasteries for themselves. It is therefore laid down that no one is to build or found a monastery or an oratory without the consent of the bishop of the city. Further, monks everywhere, both in cities and in the countryside, are to be under the authority of the bishop, devoting themselves to holy silence and giving all their attention to fasting and prayer in those places in which they renounced the world. . . .'

The canon goes on to say that the monk may on occasion undertake necessary work outside his house but only with episcopal permission. Later legislation, both ecclesiastical and imperial, constantly reaffirmed the bishop's responsibility.

Another pressing problem was to ensure the continued existence of each monastic foundation. Legislation reiterated the necessity for adequate endowment and sometimes even restricted the establishment of new houses. The iconoclasts were openly anti-monastic. With their defeat there was such a violent reaction that the council of Constantinople of 861 had to forbid bishops to found monasteries out of their revenues to the detriment of the see. Private individuals, regarding the act of foundation as a work of piety, had evidently been equally lavish. In some cases founders were treating the monastic house as their private property and freely selling or using what had been dedicated to its use, appointing their own nominee as abbot. Here again steps were taken to try and avoid what might amount to virtual secularisation. The necessity for getting the bishop's permission was emphasised and a record of authorised foundations was to be kept in the episcopal archives, while the founder was not to nominate either himself or another as head of the house without the permission of the bishop.

The hold of monasticism never diminished and after the iconoclast period until the end of the Empire it proved impossible even for imperial prohibition to control the constant donation of landed property for this purpose. In the tenth century the Emperor Nicephorus II, himself a devout and ascetic man who had once hoped to enter a hermit's cell on Mt Athos, forbad new foundations and the endowment of monasteries with land, save in certain very special circumstances. He pointed out that the essence of monasticism was not to pile up magnificent buildings and vast estates but to emulate the holy poverty of the early monastic fathers. Certain later Emperors and ecclesiastics shared Nicephorus' views, but the only effective limits ever set to the acquisition of monastic property came through the bitter experience of the Ottoman conquest.

The management of monastic temporalities raised many difficulties, partly due to the desire to honour an institution held in widespread respect, partly because monasteries themselves fell from their high calling. In spite of the exhortations of reformers, both lay and ecclesiastical, many monasteries continued to add to their possessions, and their lands might be distant and widely scattered. In some cases a steward (the ephor, or *epitropus*) was appointed to deal with such administration. Another device frequently used by the Emperor and churchmen was to grant a monastery with all its property as a *charisticum*. This meant that it would be put in charge of a 'protector', the *charisticarius*, who took over the management of the monastic lands and allowed the community sufficient for its daily needs and for the upkeep of its fabric. At its best this resulted in the sound economic development of monastic estates, but the system was open to abuse and was often criticised by ecclesiastics. Some founders specifically stated that their house was not to be granted to anyone in any circumstances, as did the Empress Irene in 1118. On the whole the practice was accepted, provided that the house kept its monastic character.

The founders of a monastery might be lay or ecclesiastical of any social rank. The eleventh-century St Dorotheus in Asia Minor built his little house himself with the aid of two or three companions and the villagers. He afterwards obtained imperial confirmation and aid. A house often had many patrons and benefactors. The founder's rights could pass to others by inheritance or agreement, sale or delegation. The house had to contain at least three monks (above this the founder might stipulate the number). Its endowments were specified in a document called a *brevion*,[1] and deposited in the episcopal archives. The *brevion* was part of the foundation charter, which also contained the founder's wishes concerning liturgical obligations (e.g. prayers for himself and his family, special rulings for fasts or festivals) and laid down the particular obligations with which the community were charged.

There were various kinds of foundation as well as the 'eparchial' house[2] directly under the diocesan. Certain houses obtained the privilege of coming directly under patriarchal control, or in the case of an autocephalous church, under its highest ecclesiastical authority.[3] Imperial houses, 'the monasteries of my Empire', were exempt from all civil and ecclesiastical authorities whatsoever, save only the Emperor or his representative.[4] Such houses were either imperial foundations or their founder had obtained this privilege for them from the Emperor. Completely independent, or *autodespotai*, houses were by the terms of their foundation withdrawn from all jurisdiction, imperial, patriarchal, episcopal, or that of private individuals. There were certain formalities connected with the founding of a monastic house. First the bishop's permission had to be given; then episcopal dedication took place with the appropriate ceremony and the planting of the cross,[5] usually at the place where the high altar was to be erected. Three years later there would be a festal procession and the announcement of the founder's arrangements for the upkeep of the house.

The necessity for testing vocation, and eliminating unworthy motives, as well as safeguarding the rights of others, made it essential to regulate entry into the monastic life. The position of slaves had to be defined; these were not to be enticed from their masters, and runaways could be reclaimed within their three-year novitiate (Justinian, *Nov.* 5), or even later than this according to Leo VI (*Nov.* 10). One party alone could not break up a marriage, nor dissolve a betrothal. In the case of both married parties entering monasteries provision had to be made for dependants, as children

---

1. From *breve*. Latin had largely been the administrative language of the East Roman Empire in its early days.
2. From *eparch* or diocese.
3. e.g. in the case of Cyprus this was the Archbishop.
4. Cf. Nicephorus II Phocas who spoke of 'the New Lavra of my Empire' in his foundation charter for the Great Lavra on Mt Athos (although called 'the Lavra' it was a cenobitic house).
5. Hence the term 'stauropegial', though this came to be applied to a monastic house under direct patriarchal control.

or parents. By the Council in Trullo (691) virgins could enter at ten years of age; Basil the Great had suggested sixteen or seventeen years. Leo VI (*Nov.* 6) said that if they entered at ten they could not dispose of their property until the later age. Provided certain obligations were fulfilled, the monastery had the right of legal inheritance, as well as the acceptance of free gifts. What had been given to the monastery as dowry, either by adults or by parents on behalf of their children, was to remain even though the individual left the house.[1] The only exception was in the case when departure was due to justifiable complaint against the superior.

The problem both of property and of monastic discipline arose in the case of the reception of a monk from another house. Justinian laid down that the property remained with the original house. At the same time heads of houses were rebuked for allowing this practice, which was condemned as being contrary to the profession of monastic life. Eastern monasticism sometimes has to bear the reproach of instability in contrast to the *stabilitas loci* so firmly enunciated by St Benedict of Nursia (though St Benedict did say that he was only providing a 'little rule for beginners' and hints that it need not necessarily bind the more experienced ascete). As a matter of fact indiscriminate wandering was never approved by Byzantine ecclesiastical authority, nor indeed by lay-founders. Conciliar and patriarchal rulings and the comments of the twelfth-century canonist Balsamon make it clear that only after proper safeguards had been observed could a monk be transferred from one house to another. Normally he had to have the permission of both superiors and of the bishop of his diocese and the change had to be made for some specific reason. In the tenth century the Lavra on Mt Athos allowed its monks to go to another superior with the consent of their former hegoumenos when this was considered to be desirable for their spiritual development. The bishop himself by the Council of 861 (canon 4) had the right to transfer a monk to another monastery if he thought this desirable.

From the early days of Egyptian monasticism there had been an initial period of probation for the novice. St Basil did not specify the length of this, though he regarded it as essential.[2] Justinian spoke of three years for slaves and unknown men, whilst others could be received by the abbot as he thought fit (*Nov.* 123). This legislation had evidently allowed some to enter on their vows too soon, and the Council of Constantinople of 861 (canon 5) laid down a three-year

1. Seventh General Council (787), canon 19.
2. *Longer Rule*, 10.

novitiate for all, except those who had lived saintly lives in the world (for whom six months sufficed) or novices (or others) who were seriously ill and might therefore be admitted to the monastic status forthwith. Apart from these exceptions, later practice often reduced the three-year period, sometimes at the abbot's discretion, sometimes by reason of the foundation charter. St Athanasius' *typicon* for the Lavra on Mt Athos specified a one-year novitiate. The order of frocking a monk or nun is to be found in the liturgical book called the *Euchologion*. The exact date when this book was compiled is not known, but the two Byzantine rites for the 'great' and 'little' habit[1] are found in early manuscripts of the eighth to ninth century. The 'great' habit was assumed by the more experienced and proved monk. The 'little' habit marked the ordinary novice's entry into the monastic life. The novice was to be received by his superior if he was a priest; if not, the ceremony was performed by a priest in the presence of the superior under whom the novice was to serve.[2]

The head of the cenobitic house was the abbot (often called hegoumenos or kathegoumenos). The manner of his election varied. He might be nominated by the founder, or by the bishop of the diocese or the patriarch. Sometimes he was chosen by the community who first nominated several candidates and then chose one of these. Details of procedure were often carefully laid down in foundation charters, for instance as to whether the vote were to be open or secret, or as to who was to have the casting vote if need arose. The election had to be confirmed by the diocesan bishop, or by the Patriarch in the case of a stauropegial house. The abbot usually held office for life, though in certain circumstances he might resign, or be deposed. He was responsible for both spiritual and temporal matters. It was he who assigned younger monks to a spiritual father, an older man who instructed them and heard their confessions, though he could only give absolution if permission to do so had been granted by the Patriarch or the ordinary; on occasion medieval monks had sometimes claimed this by virtue of a special *charisma*. The actual performance of the liturgical Office was entrusted to a group of officers each with his special duty: they woke the brethren in good time, saw that no one fell asleep or gossiped

1. The habit (*schema*) was the distinctive black garment of the monk and the symbol of monastic status. Hence the term *schematologion* for the monastic ceremonial section in the *Euchologion*. The word *schema* was sometimes used to mean 'the monastic way of life'. For a French translation of the ceremony see E. Amand de Mendietta, *La presqu'île des caloyers: île Mont-Athos* (Bruges 1955), pp. 324 ff.

2. Council of Constantinople 861 (canon 2).

during the services, superintended the ceremonial and the singing and looked after the service books.

In domestic administration the oeconomus had general charge of the economy of the house and with the help of his assistants dealt with finance, clothes, food and drink. Provision was made for the library and copying books, as also for the sick and the care of guests or the poor. Additional responsibilities might fall to the community by reason of some particular charge in the foundation charter, as the maintenance of a hospital or orphanage, or dispensation of alms at certain times. Special care was taken to assign to all some share in the daily routine. Theodore the Studite gives a lively picture of the various duties allotted to his monks in the workshops and in the fields as well as in the house itself. He made a feature of learning and copying books. To him, as to St John of Damascus, capacity to think clearly meant deeper understanding of the Bible and of the church fathers, and greater strength in the struggle against heretics.

The routine of daily life in a large and well-known house such as the Studite monastery, or St Mamas in Constantinople under Symeon, can be reconstructed, even down to minute details of the Studite menu and meals with nine monks at each table with their cowls drawn up, and their communal wardrobe with clothes changed once a week. Above all the common life was centred in the Office. These services in the monastery church at different times during the day and night were known as the liturgical hours.[1] They consisted mainly of prayers, psalms, lessons from the Bible, hymns and versicles; they varied according to the time and season. Easter for instance had its own splendid ritual and hymns, while from day to day throughout the year were commemorated the different names of those whose sanctity had won them a place in the liturgical calendar of the Eastern Church, as well as local saints who were venerated in their own district. The centre of this corporate worship was the divine liturgy, the communion service. What this worship could, and should, mean to the monk is shown by the kind of instruction on the spiritual life which was regularly given in a monastic community, and by the accounts of the personal experiences of those far advanced in the spiritual life, such as Theodore the Studite and Symeon the New Theologian.

1. Midnight prayers, Orthros, Prime, Terce, Sext, None, Vespers, Compline (Apodeipnon). See E. Wellesz, *Byzantine Music*, for a brief account of Byzantine liturgy and its content (with bibliography). Not all monks attended Terce, Sext and None on weekdays; and in Theodore the Studite's house copyists were often exempt from certain Hours.

Monastic leaders of the medieval Orthodox Church, like those of the early days, regarded the cenobitic house as the best starting point for most men. Few would have gone as far as to maintain that it was the only way. Throughout the middle ages, and after, there was great variety within the monastic framework of the Eastern Church. Houses or groups of hermits might be federated under an elected superior, often called a Protos. In Palestine in the sixth century there was one head of all the *coenobia* and one over the lavras. The houses on Mt Athos, those on Mt Latros, or the group of the Meteora in Thessaly, had their Protos. Sometimes a house would be given other monasteries as its dependencies, and often groups of cells (scetes) or individual hermitages were under a cenobitic house.

In addition to the *coenobium*, the lavra or collection of hermit groups under a superior continued. In the later middle ages the idiorrhythmic system developed, and is followed today by some of the monasteries on Mt Athos. Some assert that this was due on Mt Athos to the deterioration of the common life, partly owing to disturbances such as the Fourth Crusade or the attacks of the Catalan Company. This may have been a contributory factor, but the germ of the idiorrhythmic life was there in the early scetes and lauras. Monks in an idiorrhythmic monastery were grouped in small 'families' each under a superior. The house had certain common property administered by two or three annually elected stewards (*epitropi*). Individuals were permitted private ownership and lived in their 'family', except for a common meal at Christmas and Easter or on their patronal festival, but the Office was sung in the communal chapel.

Monastic sources illustrate the elasticity of constitutional arrangements. They illustrate too the interdependence of cenobitic and hermit life. Byzantine religious did not usually have to choose one or the other. Men often wanted to adopt a solitary life 'away in the mountains or caves' before they were ready for the experience. We have the story of an eleventh-century Latin bishop who had committed manslaughter. He came with this intention to do penance in exile in the Eastern Church, but was advised in Constantinople to be a 'solitary' within a cenobitic house where he would profit greatly from having to give up his own will.[1] It was normal to begin in the common life, and then with the approval of his superior a monk might follow the more difficult eremitic way that only the spiritually advanced could rightly undertake. Thus many cenobites were allowed

1. Nicetas Stethatus, *Vie de Syméon le Nouveau Théologien*, ch. 52–54 (ed. and trans. I. Hausherr, *Orientalia Christiana* XII, Rome 1928, pp. 68 ff.).

to withdraw from the community for this reason, sometimes to return later on. Symeon the New Theologian resigned his position as abbot in order to live in solitude. There were of course instances of men and women who became anchorites straight away. Some of these undertook particularly spectacular and demanding forms of asceticism. Stylites lived on pillars; this was not quite so precarious as often imagined. Stylites do not appear to have fallen off; there was sometimes a rail round the top of the column, or even a partial shelter erected,[1] and the top could be reached by means of a ladder. Others lived in trees and were thus called dendrites; one such is described as dwelling 'in an almond tree like a singing bird'. Continued austerity of this kind, as John Climacus and others pointed out, was beyond most men, and much monastic legislation was directed towards controlling excessive individualism which might be merely a cloak for self-indulgence and vagrancy. On the other hand those who sustained such hardships until death were deeply venerated and in their lifetime were granted supernatural graces (*charismata*) which enabled them to perform miracles and to mediate for their fellow Christians.

Throughout the middle ages monasticism remained an integral part of Byzantine life. Although many houses and anchorites had no memorial save a brief mention in chronicle or letter, there were also many well-known and old-established centres and individual houses, often in the larger cities, as Constantinople or Thessalonica and their suburbs. In Asia Minor, not far from the Sea of Marmora, Mt Olympus near Brusa was frequented from early times. Hermitages, lavras and houses were scattered on its slopes and in the vicinity, and long after they had decayed under the Turkish conquest the name 'mountain of monks' remained. Asia Minor had other such centres, as Mt Latros further south, or the monasteries and hermitages of Cappadocia now famous for their rock churches and frescoes. Greece and the Balkans, South Italy and Sicily, had their share in monastic development. Some houses in Sicily continued after the Arab conquest and were for a short time favoured by the Norman conquerors. Monasticism in South Italy was particularly flourishing, and was a refuge for Sicilians who fled there from the Arabs. The Calabrian 'Holy Mountain' was in the mountains above Rossano where today there is still a small catholicon. It was in this district that St Nilus lived before he went north to found the Greek house of Grottaferrata near Rome in 1004.

1. H. Delehaye, *Les saints stylites*, p. CLVI, on the evidence of a miniature in the *Menologion* of Basil II.

The Holy Mountain *par excellence* was Mt Athos, a peninsula of land jutting out into the Aegean near Thessalonica. There were hermits here in the ninth century. In 963 St Athanasius the spiritual father and friend of the Emperor Nicephorus Phocas made the first important cenobitic foundation with imperial support. By the mid-eleventh century every form of monastic life was flourishing and indeed in need of regulation. Mt Athos developed into a federation of houses and lavras and hermits under an elected general superior, the Protos. It enjoyed imperial protection and was greatly venerated. It attracted monks from all over the Orthodox world, and from the West. Some of its houses were specially associated with particular countries: Iviron was a Georgian (Iberian) foundation, Chilandari was Serbian, Panteleiemon was Russian (it is sometimes called Russicon), Vatopedi was Armenian, and for a time there was St Mary of the Amalfitans. The Holy Mountain had its periods of deterioration, but it was also capable of impressing the ideals of monasticism on men who went elsewhere to found other houses, as the eleventh-century St Antony of the Kievan Monastery of Caves, or the Serbians in the fourteenth century. Indeed as Byzantine political power decayed, the Holy Mountain grew in strength. From the thirteenth century onwards it experienced a far-reaching spiritual movement which was centred in the life of its contemplatives who were known as hesychasts. Some of these men were also theologians and sometimes took office in the secular church. St Gregory Palamas, one of the most experienced hesychasts, became archbishop of Thessalonica. John VI, who abdicated in 1354 and became a monk, had thought of going to the monastery of Vatopedi on the Holy Mountain (though in actual fact his plan does not seem to have materialised). It was he who wrote that the monks of Mt Athos were like Atlas because they upheld the whole world 'interceding for it with God'.[1]

Monasticism served the medieval polity in many ways. It did not have to provide education to the same extent as Latin monasticism did in the early middle ages, but it was a useful ally in the field of social services. Monks and monasteries helped to administer orphanages and hospitals; they formed funeral associations, and provided burial places for Emperor or founder, or for the unclaimed pauper's corpse; they were the refuge of the political failure and the enforced home of the criminal. The *Euchologion* has special prayers for frocking penitents sent to a monastery. Amongst those punished in this way Justinian's legislation and later canon law mention adult-

1. John Cantacuzenus, *Hist.* IV, 24 (vol. III, pp. 175–6, Bonn 1832).

eresses, deaconesses engaged in unseemly secular business, fugitive monks, any ecclesiastic, from a bishop downwards, found gambling or going to theatrical shows (who was to be incarcerated in a monastery for three years with loss of his office).[1] Chronicles abound with instances of defeated politicians, deposed Emperors, unpopular queen mothers, who 'entered' monastic houses, sometimes only to leave them again at the earliest opportunity, but more often to disappear for ever from the world. Emperors who knew that death was approaching, humbly put off their imperial robes and were received into the monastic state, rejoicing to leave the world in the plain habit of a monk.

Monasticism had its abuses; its very popularity meant that it had to fight to maintain its standards within its houses—witness the struggles of St Symeon the New Theologian. The heretics of our day, said Symeon, addressing his monks, are those who live now and cannot become like the holy fathers.

'Tell me, why is this impossible? And by what means then have the saints shone on earth and become lights in the world? If it were impossible, they too could not have achieved it. For they were men as we are. And they had no more than we have, except their resolution for good, fervour, humility and love to God. Therefore acquire this yourselves and your soul which is now stony, will become for you a spring of tears. And even if you do not wish to take the difficult and narrow way, at least do not say that such things are impossible.'[2]

Criticism and satire if taken at their face value will not explain the power of monasticism. Archbishop Eustathius of Thessalonica in the twelfth century wrote a scathing condemnation of monasticism which is often quoted as though it represented the general state of affairs. Occasionally abbots may have been chosen who could only talk about farming, but there is far more evidence to show the heights to which heads of houses could rise. It was Abbot Symeon's sermons and mystical writings which went through edition after edition from his own day to ours, and were constantly being excerpted for inclusion in anthologies, and not the agricultural sermons which Archbishop Eustathius criticised. One of the main channels for Byzantine creative experience was its spirituality. The writings of men such as Gregory of Nyssa, Evagrius of Pontus, John Climacus,

1. *Nov.* 123 and 134; Nomocanon VIII, 14 (G. A. Rhalles and M. Potles, *Syntagma* . . . vol. I, p. 161, Athens 1858).
2. *Catechesis*, 29, 164–73, quoted B. Krivocheine, 'The most enthusiastic zealot', *Ostkirch. Studien*, IV (1955), pp. 122–3.

Theodore the Studite, as well as Symeon the New Theologian and the hesychasts of the later middle ages and many others, witness to the perpetual moral struggle that lay behind their spiritual experience. These holy men spent their lives in warfare—the life of the first monk Antony makes this plain. The distress and agony that runs through Symeon's writings, his passionate awareness of his own shortcomings, are in proportion to the mystical heights which he reached through the grace of God. There was nothing passive about the holy quiet of the great contemplatives. Nor did they fail to respond to the needs of others whether by prayer or example, or by direct intervention. One of Symeon's heaviest burdens was his 'great care of all the brethren' who were with him. Gregory Palamas left Mt Athos to defend publicly the spiritual practices of the hesychasts. John of Damascus and Theodore the Studite openly supported the veneration of icons and rebuked Emperors. Icons and hesychasm were questions which were bound up with the very roots of Orthodoxy, and the spiritual life of all depended on the maintenance of right belief. Thus the monks were recognised as the pillars of the Byzantine world. They were advisers of the laity, mediators in times of bad harvest or plague or personal troubles. Villagers and townsfolk instinctively turned to the holy man, 'the friend of God, whose life of prayer brought him special graces'. In his life of an eleventh-century abbot in the countryside of Asia Minor, John of Euchaita wrote, 'The saint has the power of supplying what is lacking.'[1] It was this which accounted for the unique place of monasticism in East Roman society.

1. Migne, *Patrologia Graeca*, 120, col. 1073, *Life of St Dorotheus*.

VIII

EVERYDAY LIFE

The definitive social and economic history of the Byzantine Empire has yet to be written.[1] There is an abundance of material on which a Rostovtzeff may one day base such a history. Apart from purely theological and rhetorical works, most sources provide something. Details may be gleaned from some of the chatty letters in the papyri of the early period, from saints' lives, inscriptions and chronicles, and in the later period from monastic foundation charters, privileges and cartularies, and handbooks such as the *Gunner's Manual*, or the directions for sailors in 'the portulan books. The most substantial and valuable body of evidence is probably afforded by the public and private legal codes. By their nature these often have to provide for infringement and abnormality, but they are also full of unsuspected and often amusing detail illustrating problems of social and economic life common to every age—compensation for injury and loss of work and free medical treatment, minute building regulations concerning lights, rain pipes and gutters, preservation of public and private amenities. Private owners have the right to their direct views of the sea, gardens or public monuments, though the person claiming the right to enjoy the prospect of historical monuments, e.g. statues of such as Achilles or Ajax, must first prove that he has sufficient education to appreciate them.[2] All the same there is nothing offering

1. L. Bréhier and P. Kukules have done much to break the ground for a study of this kind, though the time for such a book has probably not yet come. Relevant material (e.g. documents, coins, seals) is still in process of being collected. It is scanty for the earlier period, but the patient editing and scrutiny of scholars such as Ostrogorsky and Dölger have demonstrated what the later sources can be made to yield on social and economic problems.

2. *A Provincial Manual of Later Roman Law: the Calabrian Procheiron*, rendered into English by E. H. Freshfield (Cambridge 1931), pp. 78–9.

the detailed wealth of economic and administrative material which is to be found in such English sources as *Domesday Book* or the *Dialogue of the Exchequer*, or the local regulations for trade and industry in individual towns, as Bristol or Southampton. But even if Byzantine changes in land tenure and in social structure on a regional basis over so long a period cannot yet be satisfactorily reconstructed, it is at least possible to indicate something of the daily round at different levels.

For the medieval East Roman Empire, as for medieval western Europe, the centre of normal life for the laity was the family. This applied to rich and poor alike, from imperial circles down to the humblest village home. Slaves and eunuchs were employed in rich families. Slavery, though discouraged by the Church, continued to the very end of the Empire. Eunuchs could rise to high office in imperial service and certain positions were reserved for them. Marriage had a prominent place in Byzantine legislation and its sanctity was stressed in both canon and imperial law. Re-marriage was frowned on: a second marriage was permitted, a third only under penalty, and a fourth incurred excommunication. Hence the difficulties of the Emperor Leo VI, who only got his heir from the mistress whom he subsequently made his fourth wife in the teeth of bitter ecclesiastical opposition. Divorce could be obtained for certain offences, and it looks from the eleventh-century *Peira* (a collection of the rulings and discussions on various cases by the judge Eustathius Romaius put together by an unknown hand) as though it was common, and even arranged by consent, which was then illegal. The position of a woman in Byzantine law was a reasonably favoured one. Her dowry was carefully safeguarded; if widowed, she was the legal guardian of her children as long as she did not re-marry and in the *Ecloga* she controlled all her husband's property 'as the head of the family and household'. If her husband was elected bishop he could only accept this office if she agreed of her own free will to leave him and go to a convent, otherwise he had to decline.[1]

Frequent stress on the need for decorous conduct in public should not be taken as implying that the life of a Byzantine woman was necessarily a secluded one—the ladies of the imperial family had prominent positions in court ceremonial, as well as opportunities for determining policy. Justinian the Great's wife urged leniency towards the monophysites; the orthodox use of icons was restored first by the Empress Irene, and then in 843 by the Empress Theodora; and Anna Comnena tells how her grandmother acted as regent

1. Isaac II Angelus, *novel* of 1187.

during the Emperor's absence from the capital and how he was accompanied on campaigns by his wife Irene. Lower down the social scale the women in the family are occasionally revealed in contemporary sources. Psellus' mother in the eleventh century was the pivot of his family circle and he owed his education to her efforts. In the life of the seventh-century Theodore of Sykeon his biographer speaks not of the saint's father, but of the women in his home—his mother who was annoyed because he did not come home from school to eat his mid-day meal, and his grandmother who had a secret sympathy with his eremitic leanings and slipped off to his chapel retreat to bring him 'a little nourishment of fruit or some vegetable salad, but this only on Saturdays and Sundays'.[1]

One can often visualise what people did and how they lived, from the Emperor down to his humblest subject. The essential Christian framework was the same for all—baptism, the penitential seasons, the festivals of the liturgical year, the Lenten fast and the Easter lamb; pilgrimages, whether to some distant and specially hallowed city as Jerusalem, or a day's excursion from the village up the mountainside to the shrine of a local saint, perhaps from Stiris along the mule-track to the monastery of Hosios Lukas. And then for each the inescapable summons from 'the Emperor of emperors' and Lord of lords, and the departure from this world, and the last rites. The most splendid pageantry was that connected with the Emperor's household, when the city would be delighted by an imperial baptism, or would mourn at an imperial funeral. Mark the Deacon describes the baptism in the early fifth century of Arcadius' heir, the baby Theodosius.[2] Constantinople was decorated with silk hangings and every kind of gold and other ornament; the streets were filled with gaily clad crowds; the procession to the church in the Palace, wearing white and looking as though snow had fallen on it, was led by patricians and high dignitaries, followed by imperial regiments all holding lighted candles so that stars seemed to shine on earth, and then came the baby carried by a noble, and near him his proud and happy father in shining purple.

Family joy or sorrow was the same in high and lowly circles. Anna Comnena mourning for her father, Psellus for his sister, share a common grief. Psellus gives a moving picture of his own numb sorrow when he arrived home to find his relations and friends at the tomb of the dead girl, whither they had returned to lament in pagan

1. E. Dawes and N. H. Baynes, *Three Byzantine Saints*, p. 98.
2. *Life of Porphyry of Gaza*, pp. 39–40 (ed. H. Grégoire and M.-A. Kugener, Paris 1930, with French trans.).

fashion on the seventh day after the funeral, a reminder of the tenacity of custom. Indeed to this very day one can still prowl round the Balkans and Greece catching glimpses of the medieval world— the Paschal lamb is carried home from market slung round the neck, and roasted whole over charcoal; candles twinkle 'like stars' on the hillside of Lycabettus as the congregation comes out of church after greeting the risen Christ in the early hours of Easter morning; or in southern Serbia food and drink are still brought to the church when prayers are offered for the dead of each family on All Souls' Eve, and early the next morning the long procession of village women and girls fetch their baskets and plates and bottles from church and carry them up to the cemetery on the hill, where some of the food is left on the graves and some is eaten. Thus has tradition survived.

Byzantine society was clearly defined but not rigidly exclusive. A peasant's son could become Emperor and an inn-keeper's daughter could marry the heir to the throne. Any clever boy could work his way to the highest post. During the heyday of Byzantium the centre of the social and imperial life was the capital: 'he who has Constantinople has the Empire'. After 1204 there were many rival attractions, as Thessalonica, Trebizond, Mistra, as well as the opportunities afforded at the courts of the Balkan princes or the Latins in Greece and the Aegean, or even in Ottoman circles. At the Byzantine court during the great days of the Macedonians in the tenth century imperial ceremonial was meticulously and magnificently executed and—however jaundiced a picture Liutprand gives of his second embassy—it was clearly most impressive. It is described in the *Book of Ceremonies*. Constantine VII states in the introduction that ceremony is an outward and visible sign of an inward harmony, and orderliness of public ritual enhances the dignity of the imperial majesty. This sense of what was fitting and appropriate was shared by his subjects. The account of the martrydom of the Forty-Two Saints of Amorium tells how the Ethiopian executioner advanced with sword outstretched and the officers presented themselves according to their rank as though at an imperial ceremony.

Sources also reveal the more human side of court life. Emperors had their relaxations. 'The holy pair', Alexius Comnenus and his wife, liked to read theological works while they had breakfast; the grim, soured Basil II had a soft spot for his second niece Zoe. Human needs in the material sense were literally catered for in little private vestries in Hagia Sophia where the Emperor and Empress were each separately served with refreshments after service in the cathedral before the formal departure. Then the Empress and her ladies would go their way to their apartments, and the Emperor would be escorted by the Patriarch to the door leading to the Holy Well.[1] Here the Emperor presented bags of gold to the clergy, and the Patriarch placed on his head the crown which he had taken off on entering the cathedral. The Patriarch too had his own rooms both in the cathedral and in his adjoining apartments where he breakfasted, and sometimes the Emperor would join him for this meal.

The food eaten in the better-off households was varied, the main dishes being of poultry and meat. 'Above all, provide a good pig for our party, but see that it *is* a good one, not a lean useless thing like the last time', wrote an Egyptian to the steward of his estate in the early period.[2] In Alexandria the patriarchal table in the early seventh century evidently offered soup, vegetables, fish, wine and oil.[3] St Theodore of Sykeon's mother ran an inn and had a very good cook who was well known for his tasty dishes; when she tried to tempt her son to eat she offered him different kinds of boiled and roasted birds and loaves of white bread.[4] The very poor lived more simply. The eleventh-century lawyer Attaliates founded monasteries charged with certain duties, amongst them that of feeding 'my brothers in Jesus Christ, the needy poor'. The food distributed to widows, the old and the infirm was bread and wine, and every day six poor men were given a meal in the monastery where they had bread, either dried or fresh cooked vegetables, meat or fish, and whatever else there might be, as well as being presented with four coppers (*folleis*). In monastic circles fish and vegetables were the rule, though even here there were exceptions. A special dispensation concerning meat was made to satisfy the outraged daughters of Constantine VII when on their father's death they were pushed into a nunnery by their unpleasant sister-in-law; Symeon the New Theologian shared a pigeon rather than cause embarrassment to a guest with gastric trouble.

In an Empire predominantly agrarian in character, local products formed the staple diet, and varied in detail from district to district. Where they were obtainable, cheeses made by the Vlach shepherds were popular. Provisioning the few big cities, especially Constantinople, was not always easy, and hence imperial care to ensure the corn supply of the capital. The tenth-century *Book of the Prefect*

1. This relic was the edge of the well where Christ met the Samaritan woman.
2. Quoted H. I. Bell, *Egypt from Alexander the Great to the Arab conquest* (Oxford 1948), p. 97.
3. E. Dawes and N. H. Baynes, *Three Byzantine Saints*, p. 230.
4. Ibid., p. 97.

describes the duties of the various guilds in Constantinople.[1] The guilds dealing with provisions were the Grocers, Bakers, Butchers (excluding pork), Pork-Butchers and Fishmongers. The prices were strictly controlled by the Prefect (or Eparch) and buying and selling were regulated. For instance fishmongers had to buy 'from the sea beach or the piers from fishing smacks at anchor' and were forbidden to undercut the market by getting cheap supplies from boats out at sea. Grocers were allowed to have their shops in the squares and streets throughout the city as they sold the necessaries of life, which included meat, salt-fish, meal, cheese, honey, olive oil, all kinds of vegetables and butter. Inns sold wine and foodstuffs, but not before 8 a.m. on great festivals or Sundays, and they had to close by 8 p.m. and put out all fires. Bakers also had to take special precautions to prevent fire. They were so essential to the city that neither they nor their animals were ever liable to be called upon for any public service.

There is of course no means of knowing exactly how strictly these regulations were applied in Constantinople, either in the early tenth century or at other times, but there is evidence that prices and profits were controlled by the state, certainly to the twelfth century. This was in the interests more of the imperial exchequer than of the consumer. Nicephorus II was reproached with making money out of buying up corn in time of famine. Attempts in the late eleventh century to profit from a state monopoly in corn had disastrous effects. What was done in Constantinople was the practice in other large cities, though certain of these, notably Alexandria and Antioch, passed out of imperial control with the Arab conquest of the mid-seventh century. In the early seventh century in Alexandria the Patriarch John expostulated at length in the council room with the patrician Nicetas who wanted 'to regulate the market so as to ensure a profit for the state, whereas the Patriarch would not tolerate this because he took thought for the welfare of the poor'.[2]

Practically nothing is left of palaces or domestic buildings of the Byzantine period, except the shell of the fourteenth-century Mistra on a spur of the Taygetus Mountains, and some remains of the imperial palace in Constantinople. This meagre evidence can be supplemented from mosaics and frescoes, and from literary sources. The Sacred Palace in the capital was a vast complex of buildings providing for the imperial retinue, and it was connected with the cathedral of Hagia Sophia. Rich families had palaces on a smaller

1. Translated by E. H. Freshfield (Cambridge 1938).
2. E. Dawes and N. H. Baynes, *Three Byzantine Saints*, p. 225.

scale with their chapels and gardens and fountains. Interiors were decorated with mosaic cycles or frescoes. Those of the Great Palace which survive are remarkable for their vigour and realism.[1] The less well-off in a big city would live in apartments, or tenements. Michael Attaliates in the eleventh century had property which he let in this way. The rich had an abundance of clothes: the fourteenth-century Theodore Metochites tells of his wife's wardrobe bulging with dresses. In the thirteenth century it was fashionable to wear Vlach capes. During the later middle ages foreign styles, particularly Italian or Turkish, were specially modish; the turban-like head-dress of the mosaic of the fourteenth-century Theodore Metochites in the church which he restored is a reminder of this, and conservatives like his younger contemporary Nicephorus Gregoras moaned because fashions were such a hotchpotch that it was impossible to pick out those who were Byzantine (*Romaioi*) among the welter of foreigners in the City. Humbler domestic details, as of spinning and weaving, kitchen utensils and plates and pots and pans, are shown in the frescoes, especially those in the Balkan churches. Occasionally something comes to light in excavations, as in the Agora in Athens where plates were found, some bearing designs illustrating the popular cycle of the Byzantine Robin Hood, Digenis Akritas, and some more simply decorated with homely little rabbits or small boys playing ball.

There were extremes of wealth and poverty. At the lowest end of the scale life was bitter and precarious and to remedy this was beyond the resources of the charitable foundations, many as they were. In the life of St John the Almsgiver there is a poignant picture of the poor in Alexandria at the beginning of the seventh century. The Patriarch John refused to sleep under a sumptuous eiderdown which was given him by a landowner who heard that he was using 'a torn and worn quilt'. Under pressure, he put the gift on his bed for one night only, moaning to himself,

'Who shall say that humble John was lying under a coverlet costing 36 nomismata whilst Christ's brethren are pinched with cold? How many are there at this minute grinding their teeth because of the cold? and how many have only a rough blanket half below and half above them so that they cannot stretch out their legs but lie shivering, rolled up like a ball of thread? How many are sleeping on the mountain without food or light, suffering twofold pangs from cold and hunger? How many would like to be filled with the outer leaves of the vegetables which are thrown away from my kitchen? How many would like to dip their bit of bread into the soup-

1. See *Illustrated London News*, 12 March 1955.

water which my cooks throw away? How many would like even to have a sniff at the wine which is poured out in my wine-cellar? How many strangers are there at this hour in the city who have no lodging-place but lie about in the market-place, perhaps with the rain falling on them?"[1]

The eiderdown was sold and the proceeds bought 144 rough blankets for the destitute.

To care for the poor was a Christian duty which fell on all, and it was one of the special obligations of the monastic world. In his foundation charter Attaliates stipulated that each monk in his house should offer part however small of his mid-day meal to a poor person. It was indeed the monks who often administered lay alms. The devout layman who founded a house usually made some special provision for the needy, the poor, the sick, and the traveller or pilgrim. The more lavish foundations established orphanages, hospitals, hospices. One of the most splendid endowments was that of John Comnenus in the twelfth century. He provided a monastery with two churches, and placed in its care not only a hospital for men and women, but homes for old men and epileptics, illegitimates and orphans, as well as one for lepers. His foundation charter sets out his intentions. There were fifty beds in the hospital, divided into five wards, one for surgical, one for medical cases, one for the use of women, and two for simple cases. Staffing was more than adequate (including one woman doctor), diet was vegetarian but well-balanced. There was a surgery and dispensary for out-patients. The sons of the medical staff had their own school where they were instructed in the rudiments of medicine. The whole institution was under the charge of the head of the monastery, though he delegated much of this to one of the choir brothers. The detail of the charter is remarkable and reads more like the twentieth century than what is commonly imagined of the twelfth. The bigger and wealthier foundations of this kind were in or near the capital, and the more remote country populations had to rely on such less specialised help as might be available in their neighbourhood. There was evidently some expert medical help available in country districts. St Theodore of Sykeon used to recommend doctors and surgeons to cases he could not deal with himself.

Cities like Constantinople or Thessalonica or Trebizond were important manufacturing and trading centres. Constantinople had its own industries, particularly the manufacture of silks and brocades and many other luxury goods, as the jewelry or ivory and enamel

1. E. Dawes and N. H. Baynes, *op. cit.*, p. 230.

E

work for which it was noted. The finest materials and certain shades of purple dye were reserved for imperial use, either for special ceremonial garments or, more rarely, to be sent as presents to some foreign court. Regulation of the silk industry and the sale of silk material had a prominent place in the *Book of the Prefect*, and the prohibition on export was not a mere formality, as Otto I's ambassador Liutprand discovered when his baggage was ransacked by customs officials and some of his purchases confiscated. There were special imperial factories in Constantinople which made silk fabrics for the use of the imperial family and the court and higher officials of Church and State. After the arrival of silkworms in Justinian's day, raw silk was cultivated, so that the Empire was no longer entirely dependent on supplies from China. Linen was also produced and sold for manufacture in Constantinople, as well as certain perfumes and aromatics, though some of these came from abroad.

In the country the vine and olive supplied local as well as urban needs. In parts of Greece and in the uplands of Asia Minor vast herds and flocks were a source of wealth: horses, camels, long-haired goats in their hundreds roamed over the pastures and uplands of the great estate whose wealth was one of the main props of the state, as long as it was controlled by a strong imperial government. Country life on a more modest scale is revealed in the legal code known as *The Farmer's Law*.[1] This depicts a village community of the small free-holders, the class whose ranks had been strengthened by the imperial policy from the seventh century onwards of granting land in return for military service passing from father to eldest son. Although *The Farmer's Law* applied to this type of community, many details of pastoral and agrarian life would be unaffected by the status of the cultivator. Here the farmer, sometimes with the help of a slave or hired labourer,[2] is shown engaged in working vineyards and fig-yards and cornland and in rearing his cattle, sheep and pigs. The code laid down penalties and rulings to cover the various contingencies which might arise—the herdsman's clandestine sale of an animal, the more accidental hazard of attack from wild beasts, the unpredictable behaviour of a sheepdog or a herd of swine. Some disasters were more difficult to deal with. Crops might be ruined, cattle killed or driven off, particularly on the eastern borders of Asia Minor where in turn Persian, Arab, and Turkish

1. Translated by W. Ashburner, *Journal of Hellenic Studies*, 32 (1912), pp. 87 ff., and by E. H. Freshfield, *Manual of Later Roman Law* (Cambridge 1927).

2. The eighth-century St Philaretes when he was reduced to 'a couple of oxen, a horse, a donkey, a cow and her calf' still had one slave and one servant, *Byzantion*, 9 (1934), p. 115.

(and on occasion Christian) raiders were a perpetual menace. Many small fortified homesteads on the borders inevitably fell into enemy hands and with the contraction of the frontiers were permanently lost. At all times drought, cloud-bursts, locusts and other pests might destroy the harvest and make it difficult for the farmer to pay the tax-collector. Sometimes the villagers appealed to a holy man, if there was one in the vicinity. St Theodore of Sykeon's prayers averted disaster from 'beetles, locusts, worms and dormice which were devouring the crops and the vines', and he cured oxen and other domestic animals. It was a precarious and marginal existence, and the exchange of his freedom for the lower status of tenant-cultivator (*paroikos*) with certain obligations on a large estate, whether lay or monastic, must often have seemed the only solution to the small farmer. It was otherwise with the more substantial properties where there were reserves to draw upon. Land remained one of the best investments and the great magnates flourished to the end.

The Empire had an extensive coast line and innumerable islands, and many Byzantines gained their livelihood by sea, some as fishermen, others as sailors in the mercantile marine, or in the imperial navy, at least until the rise of the Italian maritime republics from the twelfth century onwards. The code called the *Rhodian Maritime Law* is a collection of regulations for small merchant ships which describes the authorised arrangements for crew and passengers. For instance, each was allowed so much space (a male passenger was given three times as much room as a woman). Many were the dangers to be guarded against, from fire on board to capture by pirates or shipwreck. Passengers were expressly forbidden to chop wood or 'to fry fish on board, and the captain shall not permit it';[1] they were however each entitled to one measure of water and could get food from the cook in charge of the little canteen. The captain could abandon passengers ashore if it was necessary to put to sea at once to avoid being plundered by pirates. Sometimes all, or part, of the cargo had to be jettisoned. One of the features of the *Rhodian Law* was its system of mutual indemnity and assurance embodying some of the principles of modern maritime insurance.[2] Trade often meant a sea journey at some point, and maritime traffic ranged from the limited activities permitted to the monks of Mt Athos to those of the fleet of the Patriarch of Alexandria which fetched tin from 'the islands of Britain' in the seventh century, or the

1. *Rhodian Maritime Law*, trans. E. H. Freshfield in *A Manual of Later Roman Law* (Cambridge 1927), p. 206.
2. See E. H. Freshfield, *op. cit.*, p. 60.

merchant enterprises ranging as far afield as India or China which
are revealed in surviving Jewish documents.[1]

Byzantines had their pastimes and amusements, their human
failings and weaknesses. The public baths were the equivalent of
clubs, where they could meet and sit chatting through the day. They
often combined business and pleasure on their pilgrimages or at
fairs. Salesmen would haunt the well-visited shrines of popular
saints. Business dates were made in the sanctuary; sometimes people
slipped out of church before the service had ended to talk outside
(and on one occasion were much disconcerted when the Patriarch
came out too, saying that as their shepherd and pastor his place was
with them). Superstition abounded in town and country: there were
charms and amulets to ward off mishap and to cure disease, including Christian prophylactics for the same purpose. John Italus
wrote to the dean of the faculty of medicine in Constantinople that
he would have no need of the usual remedies, purgatives, changes of
air, and the like, if only he wore the medallion of Constantine which
he was sending him. Villages had their wise woman or enchantress.
In more sophisticated circles séances were held; there were instructions for covering an awkward situation when a medium had con-
jured up the wrong god or an evil spirit, or when the wrong answer
had been given. Here Byzantium drew on the magical beliefs and
practices of Late Antiquity. It is evident that there was a strong
interest in spiritualist activities in East Roman circles, and medieval
experiences appear to have had much in common with modern
psychical research.[2] The Church continually frowned on all activities
of this kind, including astrology. In his *Fount of Knowledge* John of
Damascus bluntly attacked the claims of astrologers and pointed
out that stars or climate could not determine a man's temperament
or control all our affairs. 'We have been created with free wills by
our Creator and are masters over our own actions.'[3] The Quini-
Sextum Council[4] of 691 forbade pagan celebrations on May-day or

1. See the excellent article of S. D. Goitein, 'From the Mediterranean to
India: documents on the trade to India, South Arabia, and East Africa from
the eleventh and twelfth centuries', *Speculum* 29 (1954), pp. 181 ff. Though dealing primarily with Jewish trade from Cairo, these papers reveal an 'international
outlook' and throw light on medieval commerce with the Far East in general.

2. Both Graeco-Roman and Byzantine material have so far been only partially
explored. One of the best introductions to this subject is E. R. Dodds, 'Theurgy
and its relationship to neoplatonism', *Journ. Rom. Stud.* 37 (1947), pp. 55 ff.

3. John of Damascus, *De fide orthodoxa*, c. 7 (transl. *Nicene and Post Nicene
Fathers* 9 [1899], p. 24).

4. So-called because its rulings were considered to be supplementary to the
Fifth and Sixth General Councils.

at the wine harvest, as well as certain magical practices, though with what success is doubtful. The frequency of conciliar and other ecclesiastical protests of this kind shows the persistence with which age-long customs and superstitions survived. This was particularly the case in the islands, which have kept their own individual traditions and folklore almost to the present day.

Seed-time and harvest allowed little time for relaxation, and country pleasures were usually those connected with the various seasons, as the celebrations at the time of the grape harvest. These would be supplemented by occasional diversions from outside, such as a travelling troupe of acrobats on camels, or jugglers, perhaps with mimes and buffoons. In the bigger towns there was a dearth of anything corresponding to the drama of classical Greece or of modern times. There were revues and cabaret shows (which ecclesiastics were not supposed to attend). One thirteenth-century Patriarch of Constantinople (who had a 'Lenten' outlook) tried, like others before him, to have performances on Saturday and Sunday banned. The entertainment *par excellence*, the cup-tie matches of the middle ages, were the races held in Constantinople in the Hippodrome and patronised by royalty. Here the rival factions spurred on their favourites, and the triumph of the victor was identified with the triumph of the invincible Christian Emperor who often presided from the imperial box.

As in any age, there was much in everyday Byzantine life which was scurrilous and superstitious and unpleasant. But the over-all picture was one neither of decadence nor of despair. Men laughed at their doctors and lawyers and churchmen, but their very satire marked their sense of security in their heritage rather than the reverse. Until the thirteenth century they had better social services, both state provided and voluntary, and a higher standard of life in their middle and upper classes than anywhere else in Christendom. And poverty was redeemed by a realisation of the divine purpose— witness the faith of the country folk in the mediation of the holy man; trials and disaster, though doggedly combated, were recognised as a salutary discipline. In the fourteenth century when the Empire was tried beyond endurance, Nicephorus Gregoras wrote, 'Good fortune rarely smiles on us, and when it comes it withers as quickly as a flower, but this is by the will of God that we may be rightly chastened, otherwise we might get above ourselves and forget that we are only mortal.'[1]

1. Nicephorus Gregoras, *History* XVI, 4 (vol. II, p. 819, Bonn 1830).

IX

LEARNING AND LITERATURE:
THE DIFFERENT TRADITIONS

Byzantine society was an educated society, at least in its middle and upper reaches. Here, as with political and administrative tradition, there was no break with the Graeco-Roman world. Pillars of the Christian Church such as St Basil and St Gregory Nazianzus went to the university of Athens together with their pagan contemporary, Julian the Apostate. At almost the same time St John Chrysostom was thundering to parents on the right upbringing of Christian children, but whatever safeguards he might advocate to prevent their contamination by non-Christian custom and behaviour he never suggested that they should remain uneducated. Thus the early Byzantine state was the conscious heir of the literature and thought and instruments of learning of the late Roman Empire: it did not have to build up anew as did some of the younger western kingdoms. And so in the sixth century when England and France had little to offer, and practically nothing that did not come through the Church, the Byzantine Emperor was setting up commissions of jurists whose work was to influence in varying degree almost every country in Europe, and was regulating students' rags in the law-schools in terms reminiscent of modern university life. Procopius, the aide-de-camp of Justinian's general Belisarius, was writing copious volumes on war and peace, and probably at the same time relieving his feelings by composing a private account of his contemporaries (with the Emperor in the leading role) which was so injudicious, not to say libellous, that it was not published until after his death. Romanus the Melodus was composing, in what would then have been called the modern metre, antiphonal hymns which are still used today, and are hard to beat for beauty of style and content. Paul the Silentiary was writing in one of the metres of the classical world his descriptive poems on the newly built cathedral in Constantinople, the church of the Holy Wisdom, Hagia Sophia.

Throughout the Byzantine middle ages, as in the ancient world, education for the better-off was taken for granted and great store was set on writing well and speaking well. Girls as well as boys were educated; they did not usually attend universities, but higher education was evidently available for them in families which could afford private tutors. Constantine VII had a secretariat of learned daughters; the historian and soldier Nicephorus Bryennius was married to an accomplished authoress, the Princess Anna Comnena; Theodore Metochites' daughter Irene had an acute and penetrating mind and her male contemporaries observed that her conversation reminded them of Plato and Pythagoras. And not quite so high in the social scale there were instances of educated women, such as Michael Psellus' mother in the eleventh century, and the woman doctor mentioned in connection with John Comnenus' twelfth-century hospital.

Primary instruction was provided in towns, and sometimes in village schools, such as that which the seventh-century St Theodore of Sykeon went to in the countryside of Galatia in Asia Minor. Wealthier children were usually taught by tutors. Higher education was available from various sources. After an elementary education in Constantinople the ninth-century Leo the Mathematician learnt from a teacher of philosophy and mathematics on the island of Andros, and in turn himself set up as a coach in Constantinople. It was generally possible to find a private tutor for advanced studies, however low the fires of learning were reputed to be. In the early eleventh century John Mauropous instructed a brilliant group of young men who afterwards had distinguished careers; he taught for the love of his subject and asked no fee from those who could not afford it, so he writes in a moving poem about his early life in Constantinople. Sometimes a start was made in the households of patrons of learning, often themselves scholars of repute.

Then there were the well-known academies with an international reputation. The great schools of the classical period, Athens, Alexandria, Beirut, run on well into early Byzantine days, overlapping with the more recent foundation of Constantinople. Constantine the Great is known to have encouraged learning in his new capital and a centre of higher studies grew up during the second half of the fourth century. The university was formally inaugurated by Theodosius II in 425. It was established in the auditorium of the Capitol and was clearly well under imperial control. There were three orators and ten grammarians for Latin and ten grammarians and five sophists for Greek, as well as one professor of philosophy and two 'to expound the law and statutes'. Athens was closed during Justinian's reign, though this did not mean the complete cessation of learning there; Alexandria, Antioch and Beirut passed into Muslim hands, but their tradition was carried on by Constantinople which remained the best known medieval Greek centre of learning, at least until 1204. The Latin chairs there were gradually reduced in number, and finally disappeared as Latin passed out of use and the western half of the Empire was irretrievably lost. The university was the training ground of civil servants and administrators, and was usually supported by the state financially, as well as in other ways. Its history cannot always be reconstructed for lack of sources, but it appears to have flourished most in the fifth and sixth centuries and then again from the mid-ninth to the end of the twelfth century. One of the fullest surviving documents is the constitution of the Law faculty which was drawn up in 1045 when the university was reorganised by Constantine IX at the instigation of an enthusiastic and influential group of scholars. After 1204 interest to some extent shifted, first to Nicaea, and then to the Peloponnese where the Byzantine humanists attracted and taught younger scholars. There were, too, such centres as Thessalonica, or Trebizond, which maintained their cultural activities. Constantinople, however, recovered something of its former brilliance in the days of Andronicus II and Cantacuzenus, when considerable work was done, particularly in certain sciences, while public debates and disputations reflected the impact of western dialectic and theology on the jealously preserved traditions of orthodox spirituality.

Throughout its history Byzantium honoured both its private and its public teachers and regarded learning as an excellent thing, not only for princes, who had special need of it, but 'for all the rest, as well, who are subjects'.[1] Anna Comnena was particularly scornful of those who had missed, or not responded to, their training in the art of speaking and writing well; when Bishop Leo of Chalcedon fell into heresy, after all what could one expect, she asked, for 'he was incapable of making a precise statement with conviction as he was absolutely untrained in the science of reasoning'.[2] Even to the end, Byzantines kept their lively sense of the value of education, and

1. Constantine VII, *De Administrando Imperio* (ed. G. Moravcsik and trans. R. J. H. Jenkins), p. 49.
2. Anna Comnena, *Alexiad*, V. 2 (trans. E. A. S. Dawes, p. 119).

in the distressing uncertainties after the Fourth Crusade, the thir-teenth-century Emperor Theodore II of Nicaea could say 'Whatever the needs of war and defence, it is essential to find time to cultivate the garden of learning.'

The content of Byzantine education betrays its classical parentage. Primary instruction consisted of reading and writing and the study of ancient Greek literature. A quotation from Homer was recognised by Byzantines as readily as a quotation from Shakespeare used to be by us. The groundwork of elementary studies was a prelude to special training in rhetoric, followed by law or philosophy at univer-sity level, together with such subjects as medicine, arithmetic, geometry, astronomy and music. Advanced theological studies were not provided by the university of Constantinople. There were a number of ecclesiastical schools, including the patriarchal academy in the capital with its various centres attached to the different churches there. It was at one of these, the school in the church of the Holy Apostles, that Cyril the Apostle to the Slavs taught in Photius' day. Although there were no chairs in theology in the university, laymen were often competent theologians, as Photius himself and his younger contemporary Leo VI, or Manuel II in the early fifteenth century. The boundary between lay and ecclesiastical spheres of interest was almost non-existent.

Intellectual and literary activity of some kind can be found at any period in the Byzantine Empire but much of this still remains unprinted or unexplored. For instance, a satisfactory history of its sciences and learning, technology and craftsmanship, has yet to be written. To comment on the progress of Byzantine studies in certain fields is beyond the present writer. There may have been develop-ments in medicine and surgery; the writings of the sixth-century Alexander of Tralles or the early seventh-century Paul of Aegina suggest that Byzantium was the link between the school of Galen and later developments in Italy and in the Muslim world. There was certainly activity in mathematics and astronomy, such as the work of Leo the Mathematician in the ninth century, or renewed interest in the thirteenth and fourteenth centuries when the Indian decimal system came into use (this seems to appear for the first time in Byzantium in a twelfth-century scholium on Euclid).[1] Interest in astronomy was particularly strong, and added stimulus came from Trebizond which had links with Persia in the late thirteenth century.

1. On the sciences in Byzantium the reader is referred to the chapter by K. Vogel in the revised edition of the *Cambridge Medieval History* **IV**, pt. II.

Certain branches of mathematics were closely allied to philosophical studies. Indeed some scholars, like Michael Psellus, regarded mathematics as valuable simply because it afforded a link between material objects and abstract thought. In the fourteenth-century revival of higher mathematics it was one of the complaints of Theodore Metochites, statesman and scholar, that he found only those parts of Euclid and Nicomachus being studied which had some bearing on philosophy.

Philosophy was also intimately connected with theology, partly because the fathers of the early church were steeped in the thought of the ancient world. In the eighth century the first part of John of Damascus' *Fount of Knowledge*, a handbook of Christian teaching, was characteristically devoted to the logic and metaphysics of Aristotle. Interest in philosophical studies varied, and it was recognised that it called for discretion, as an enthusiast like John Italus found to his cost. It was generally regarded as a discipline which must be subordinated to Christian doctrine. But the methods and arguments of philosophy were used and found invaluable, particularly in the theological controversies of the earlier period up to the time of John of Damascus. Thus certain basic principles and works were preserved and passed on to the West. The emphasis of the revival of learning in Constantinople from the mid-ninth century onwards was humanist and literary, rather than philosophical, until the mid-eleventh century, when Aristotle, Plato, and particularly the neo-platonists were brought to the fore and vigorously studied by Michael Psellus, for a time head of the faculty of philosophy in the reorganised university. Even so, though his old friend John Xiphilinus reproachfully said that he attached too much weight to his Plato, Psellus was ready to admit that philosophy, the crowning glory of secular studies, could not be regarded entirely in its own right, but was a preparation for theology. This attitude sometimes damped philosophical speculation. Whether anything new emerged it is as yet difficult to say. There exist many glosses and commentaries on authorities such as Plato and Aristotle or the later fifth-century Proclus. It is possible that these accumulations of the medieval centuries may also prove to be of value in tracing the development of philosophical thought in the West. It is for instance known that Thomas Aquinas used John Philoponus' commentaries on Aristotle. But much is still unprinted, and Byzantine philosophy, like its other sciences, needs further investigation.

Interest in the literature of classical Greece meant that considerable time was devoted to textual and philological work. Energy was lavished on reference works, dictionaries, grammars, encyclopaedias, commentaries, anthologies, which contain a mine of information, historical and literary as well as linguistic. Eustathius of Thessalonica's twelfth-century commentary on Homer is still used by classical scholars. Photius' *Library* contains, together with his shrewd comments on all and sundry, extracts from books he had read, many of which are no longer extant. Such writings were not literary creations, but they were the essential tools and the products of an educated public.

Byzantium had also inherited from its forebears a passionate devotion to rhetoric which coloured its educational system and its literary output. Rhetoric was the discipline which enabled the writer, or speaker, to present his material in the most elegant and appropriate form, and its immediate roots were in the pagan sophistry of the Hellenistic period. Letters, panegyrics, edifying advice (as a *Mirror for Princes*), occasional pieces, orations of every kind, were poured out. Writers who had no sense of style were frowned on; the first version of the life of the ninth-century St Joannicius bitterly disappointed contemporaries because it was not elegantly expressed.

There was in fact a gulf between the written and spoken language. By the early centuries A.D. the various dialects of the classical world had merged into a 'common' language, the *koine*, which was used in the Hellenistic world. This had predominantly Attic characteristics and it underwent further modifications during the middle ages, forming the basis of modern Greek. Educated Byzantine circles did not use this living language which was their vernacular. They reverted to Attic, trying to write in the language of Thucydides or some other classical author. This was part of their conscious pride in being the guardians and possessors of ancient Greek culture, but it had unfortunate results. Often their writings were full of antiquarian terms and expressions, and sometimes grammatical errors when ancient and 'modern' usages were unwittingly combined. The church did not use the vernacular either; but much of its literature was in a simple *koine*, as distinct from the Attic of antiquity, and it developed a style of its own, particularly in its liturgical poetry and its mystical works. Indeed it sometimes used the modern quantitative rhythmic verse. Other literature occasionally inclined towards the vernacular, even in the early period, as the chronicles. The saints' lives, too, were sometimes written in a simpler language, especially in their original form before they were remodelled in what was considered to be a more literary style and perhaps embellished with quotations from Homer or some other favourite writer. They were really the equivalent of our novels, particularly in the early middle ages, and they provided an abundant supply of stories in which edification, homely detail and Arabian nights phantasy were mingled, especially in the stories of the holy men in the eastern reaches who even wandered as far afield as the shores of the Ganges. From the twelfth century onwards the spoken language began to be used in secular poems and in verse romances. And in the provinces and islands away from imperial circles Greek imagination and love of story-telling found an outlet in popular ballads and folk-poetry, only the remnants of which have survived. Although the demotic never ousted the 'pure' language in the middle ages, it was the living speech of the Greeks and after a bitter struggle it eventually came into its own in modern Greece.

Criticism has been levelled against Byzantine literature on the ground that it often consisted of wordy rhetorical works written in artificial imitation of Attic Greek. It is true that much is mediocre and disappointing, both in the 'pure' language and in the demotic, but that is not peculiar to Byzantium. Remembering the earlier glories of the classical period, critics are perhaps disappointed because Byzantine literature did not produce another Sophocles or Aristophanes. But Byzantium did not appear to be interested in a living drama, either secular or religious; in that line its tastes ran to mimes and cabarets. Its literary achievements lay elsewhere. In the field of poetry, apart from the demotic verse, there are one or two long descriptive works, as the seventh-century George of Pisidia's encomium on Heraclius, but in almost every generation short poems in the classical metre, epitaphs, descriptive lines, lyrics, and love poetry can be found. These 'epigrams'[1] are characterised by brilliance and wit, and in imagery and content often bear a close resemblance to seventeenth-century poetry. Perhaps the Cavalier poets knew their *Greek Anthology*. The popular epic was *Digenis Akritas* which sang the stirring life and robust independence of the marcher-lord born and bred in the 'mixed' culture of the eastern frontier; it roused the imagination of subsequent generations and stimulated cycles of popular ballads in Slav as well as in Greek lands. In the later middle ages, long verse romances appear in the vernacular, influenced by Frankish chivalry as well as by the Greek epic tradition.[2]

Byzantium particularly excelled in two quite different fields—in

1. So they are usually called, but the word is misleading; it is used to cover a wide range of poetry.
2. Byzantine, like Hellenistic, poetry has yet to find its F. J. E. Raby or Helen Waddell.

history and in writings specifically concerned with the Christian faith and worship.

The Byzantines were always conscious of their past, and their thought was tempered by this awareness of historical continuity. Medieval Greek historians admired the style and method of their ancestors, particularly Herodotus and Thucydides, and in the later period were also influenced by their more immediate predecessors, such as the sixth-century Agathias. History, 'the finest invention of the Greeks',[1] was no mere chronicle. 'History,' wrote Nicephorus Gregoras, 'is concerned with . . . the past and the present and with the actions of men, with the views of the learned on the nature of things, and the error or truth of such views.'[2] The quality of Byzantine historiography varied; its writers did not of course achieve perfect imitation of a Thucydides or of a Xenophon, but they did produce a number of first-rate works. Authors such as Leo the Deacon and Anna Comnena in the middle period, Nicephorus Gregoras and John Cantacuzenus in the fourteenth century, offer mature and markedly individual histories which could only have been produced in a highly cultivated society. Together with the histories properly speaking, there were also the world chronicles written for a more popular audience. These would record important events in chronological order, adding a plentiful interlarding of sensational horrors and other items of news likely to appeal to a wide public. They reflect contemporary taste and mentality, but they were not creative achievements as the histories were.

Devotion to the Christian faith inspired the other branch of literature in which Byzantines were outstanding. Here their work falls into two different categories—theological on the one hand, and ascetical and liturgical on the other. In the latter there is an added interest in that new ground is sometimes broken in adapting Greek literary forms to the special needs of the Church.

The most distinguished theological work is that of the pioneers in the early patristic period. These church fathers were immeasurably aided by the flexibility of the Greek language and the long tradition of philosophical thought. Using what was relevant in Plato, Aristotle, the Stoics, and the neo-platonists, they tried to relate man's ordered destiny in time and space to the Incarnation and to define the nature of the Godhead. A constant succession of

1. Nicetas Choniates, *History* (Bonn 1835), p. 768.
2. Nicephorus Gregoras, *Roman History*, I, 1 (vol. I, p. 4, Bonn 1829). Cf. T. A. Hart, 'Nicephorus Gregoras: historian of the hesychast controversy', *Journ. Eccles. History* 2 (1951).

later Byzantine theologians built on the patristic foundations which had been so brilliantly laid, though for lucidity and profundity only John of Damascus can stand beside an Athanasius or a Gregory of Nyssa.

In the age of the patristics towards the end of the fifth century the *Corpus Dionysiacum* was written by the so-called Pseudo-Dionysius the Areopagite. Like the fathers, it is indebted to a non-Christian past and owes much to the neo-platonists, particularly Plotinus, though it was accepted as the work of Dionysius the Areopagite, a personal follower of St Paul. It was extensively glossed by the seventh-century Maximus the Confessor, and was an important, though by no means the only, influence on later Orthodox spirituality. Byzantine ascetics were concerned to work out the implications of Christian doctrine and to develop the teaching of the Christian ascent towards deification. One of the most vital figures was that of the early eleventh-century Symeon the New Theologian. His personality made a deep impression on contemporaries, lay and ecclesiastical, and his numerous writings explain why. They are also of linguistic interest, because in his *Loves of the Divine Hymns*, where he describes his own intimate spiritual experiences, he uses modern fifteen-syllable political verse and not the classical quantitative metre. Some of his writing is of rare beauty, both in expression and content. His hymns and sermons (*orationes*) reveal the creative nature of Byzantine religious thought. It is indeed writings of this kind which provided an outlet for depth of feeling and lyrical qualities which have been expressed at other times in a secular idiom.

The same quality is found in the liturgy, whether the term is used for the communion service or for the different parts of the Office. In stressing the act of worship, the literary debt is sometimes overlooked. Parts of the service were written before the medieval period, as the psalms or lessons. But it is to the days of the early church and the early medieval period that Greek Christendom owes the solemn magnificence of the divine liturgy itself. In particular the varied beauty of the hymns which were continually being added, at least until the late eleventh century, is a further witness to the genius of the Greek language. As with some ascetical works, the poetry of the liturgical office was not written in the accepted quantitative classical metres but was rhythmic and accentual. This poetry ranged from a simple verse or short hymn to the longer dramatic hymn-sermons (*kontakia*) derived from Syriac sources and introduced by Romanus the Melodus in the sixth century, and it finally culminated in the elaborate cycle of nine hymns, known as a canon. Apart from those hymns which were incorporated into the liturgical books and are still used today (often in a truncated form), there were many collections which served as unofficial supplementary hymn-books in monastic circles. Romanus' Nativity hymn 'Today the Virgin', which legend says that the Mother of God inspired him to improvise in the pulpit of Hagia Sophia one Christmas Eve, or the Akathistos hymn in honour of the Virgin, the special protector of Constantinople, perhaps also by Romanus, show the dramatic tension of the narrative and the lyrical quality of the praise which place the *kontakia* in the first rank of medieval poetry.

Thus Byzantium, no less than the West, had its literary masterpieces. Like western countries, it too had a learned and a popular language. This medieval linguistic dichotomy has been unduly blamed for its retarded modern literary development, in reality more probably due to the unhappy political circumstances of the Greeks after 1453 and complicated by the unfortunate modern struggle over the use of the vernacular with all its political implications. Few critics are seriously disturbed because Bede did not write in Anglo-Saxon, or Aquinas in Italian, and it seems unreasonable to take offence because John of Damascus or John Cantacuzenus did not use the demotic. The pride of place which medieval Byzantium gave to the classics of antiquity both in education and in scholarship ensured their use in libraries throughout the Empire, in academies, in schools, churches and monasteries, and in the houses of private individuals. Thus in the middle ages the achievements of the classical world in the different branches of practical and theoretical knowledge were available to the East Roman, and to some extent to his neighbours. The Muslims had no inhibitions in drawing on this, though often through devious sources. The Slavs also inevitably came into close contact with Greek civilisation. The Latins, through the early patristic translations, and then through Sicily, Italy and Spain and latterly from the Aegean itself, built up their knowledge of Greek antiquity, so that when Byzantium was finally submerged in Islam, the West took over its rôle.

X

BYZANTINE ART

Byzantine art, like Byzantine history, had its roots in a Graeco-Roman world centred in the East Mediterranean. Its character was largely determined by two factors—Christianity and the imperial tradition. But the details and peculiarities of its idiom were often derived from beyond its eastern confines. There was a lively two-way interchange of ideas and methods between Byzantium and its fringe of oriental neighbours, far more so in the field of art than in literature or administration.

In the past Byzantine art has particularly suffered from the failure to appreciate Byzantine history and civilisation. Today there still remain two obstacles in the way of understanding what is now acknowledged to be one of the supreme achievements of medieval Byzantium. Appreciation of Byzantine art is not merely a subjective process; it involves knowledge of various traditions and of technical processes as well as of the historical framework in which these developed. Further, first-hand acquaintance with most of the monuments is beyond the reach of many. The interested reader can read the history of Psellus and gain a good deal, even from a translation. But no reproduction can convey precisely the effect of light striking a curved mosaic surface; and few can live in the shadow of the church of the Martorana in Palermo or of Daphni near Athens, studying their mosaics as they vary from hour to hour in the changing light.[1] Moreover, all too few monuments remain to illustrate a

1. It is of course possible to learn a good deal of the techniques involved and the results achieved from recent books on the subject, and those cited in the bibliography provide reproductions of almost everything mentioned in this chapter.

wide range of output over a long period, even though exciting dis-
coveries are still being made, as the mosaics being uncovered in
Hagia Sophia in Constantinople or the mural cycle found in a small
church in the Macedonian hills.[1]

The contrast between the architecture of the Parthenon on the
Acropolis of Athens and the cathedral of Hagia Sophia of Constantinople, between a sculptured classical figure of Apollo and the
mosaic of Christ the All-Powerful in the dome of a Byzantine church
such as that of Daphni, reflect the differing need and idiom of the
ancient world and the Byzantine Empire. The transition took place
in the later Roman Empire. Before ever Constantine the Great
became Christian two factors of significance in Byzantine art were
already apparent. Art forms were widely used to magnify the
Emperor: these range from the magnificence of the flowing narrative
on Trajan's column still standing in Rome to the legends and figures
on the coins and medallions designed to reach a wide public. And
men, no longer rejoicing in their own powers and creations but
moved, sometimes by profound pessimism, sometimes by deep
nostalgia for a regeneration and a supernatural life, whether obtained by pagan or by Christian means, were ready to see in art a
medium whereby the permanent values of a transcendental world
might be symbolised.

The Graeco-Roman use of art in the service of the ruler continued
unbroken throughout the medieval period. Constantine's triumphal arch in Rome, still more Justinian's mosaic panel in San Vitale
in Ravenna, exalt the Autocrator, Christ's vicegerent, and the very
majesty of the Pantocrator, whose mosaic came to occupy the
dominating place of honour in the cupola of Byzantine churches,
reminded men of the dignity of His representative on earth. Imperial
triumphs were recorded in mosaic on palace walls (though now
known only through literary references), on ivories and coins, and
even on textiles. Likewise pagan motifs and subjects continued—
scenes from mythology on tombs, or on ivory caskets, or in churches,
as for instance the river god of Jordan who keeps John the Baptist
company in the fifth- and sixth-century mosaics in the baptisteries
of Ravenna. Many motifs and much in the style and media of the
art of the late Empire had already come to the Graeco-Roman
world from the East. Thus, apart from direct contact with its neighbours, Byzantium inherited from Rome an art which contained both
oriental and Greek elements. Within the Hellenistic world there were
different styles and schools, as the Alexandrine with its emphasis on

1. I am indebted to Dr Kosić of Skopje for this information.

F

realism and a three-dimensional presentation, or that of Asia Minor and Syria with a greater stress on a symbolical two-dimensional picture suspended as it were *sub specie aeternitatis*.

These two different ways of representing a subject can be seen in mosaics of the fourth and fifth centuries in Italy. In S. Maria Maggiore in Rome the late fourth-century mosaics high up in the nave consist of small panels portraying stories from the Old Testament, Moses and Joshua, Abraham to Joseph. Copied from illustrations in manuscripts of the Septuagint (the Greek translation of the Hebrew Old Testament), they are not adapted to monumental use and are much too small to be seen easily. Only binoculars or the use of scaffolding reveals the subtle use of colour shading more suited to a book than the walls of a church. The scenes are faithfully represented in a naturalistic style, with foreground and distance. In contrast is the sixth-century nave of S. Apollinare Nuovo in Ravenna decorated on either side with saints and martyrs, not divided up into panels, but showing in the detachment of the long procession and in the frontality of the faces the contrasting Asiatic preference for a two-dimensional and less naturalistic representation. Both these trends can be observed in Byzantine art throughout its long life.[1]

Comparatively little is known about Byzantine secular buildings and not much has survived apart from underground cisterns and fragments such as the Tower of Tefkour Serai in Constantinople (variously dated, Grabar suggests the Palaeologan period), or the fourteenth-century imperial palace on the slopes of Mistra in the Peloponnese. Excavations in Constantinople have revealed part of the Great Palace, including a mosaic floor, probably of the mid-fifth century, with racy pictures of everyday life, such as a boy about to trap a hare which is unconcernedly nibbling a bunch of grapes, or a perverse-looking mule violently discarding rider and two bundles of sticks.

The large-scale monuments which still exist are churches, as might

1. Readers should perhaps be warned that it is not always easy to fathom the inner significance of Byzantine (and late Roman) representation, and even experts can be at a loss. For instance in a church at Nicopolis in Greece there are sixth-century floor mosaics of landscape and scenes from country life, as fishing or hunting, and in one mosaic there are two particularly large figures of hunters. Only an inscription enables one pavement to be identified as a map of the earth and ocean, which the expert admits that he might otherwise have taken for paradise. What appears to be a hunting scene is however probably paradise, while the two hunters are to be interpreted as Enoch and Elijah, symbolising the perpetual fight of virtue against vice. Cf. E. Kitzinger, 'Studies on Late Antique and Early Byzantine Floor Mosaics', *Dumbarton Oaks Studies* 6 (Cambridge, Mass. 1951).

be expected, since the faith which they were built to serve still lives. The recognition of Christianity in the fourth century and its growing ascendancy in the Empire were followed by the reconstruction of innumerable churches and monasteries. This made demands on architects and artists, all the more so since the Christian Church was generously supported by all, from the Emperor who could build and embellish a cathedral to the humblest villager who shared in the foundation of a new monastery or chapel in his neighbourhood. Side by side with the development of liturgy and ritual went not only architectural activity but the production of textiles, enamels, ivories, metal work—in fact considerable stimulus was given to all the arts which were used either to decorate ecclesiastical interiors or to provide beautiful equipment for the actual performance of the services, as vestments or vessels. Most important of all was the use of interior wall-space for purposes of interpretation as distinct from mere decoration. In this respect the art of the western medieval Church has been contrasted with that of Byzantium: the one is said to stir the feelings of the beholder, the other to be a commentary on the Christian faith. It is even possible to go further and maintain that Byzantine art is part of the congregation's act of worship.

The fourth to the sixth century was the formative period in Byzantine architecture. Existing buildings, such as the Hellenistic basilica, were adapted to Christian use. The Christian basilica had a courtyard (atrium), an antechamber (narthex), and then the nave, the main body of the church, with pillars dividing off two side-aisles and at the east end an apse. Round the apse were seats for the clergy, in front of this was the altar over relics of the martyrs, and in the nave was an ambo ascended by steps for preaching. The roof was flat. Churches of this kind in Rome are S. Maria Maggiore, or the remains of S. Maria Antiqua, or the upper church of San Clemente, which has certain features taken from an earlier church, as the ciborium. This early Christian type is also found in Greece (e.g. St Demetrius of Thessalonica, now reconstructed after being damaged in two world wars), in the Balkans and in the coastal areas of Asia Minor. Some early churches were built on a round ground plan; sometimes they were converted mausoleums, as the fourth-century S. Costanza in Rome, which was probably adapted for use as a Christian baptistery.

The architecture most characteristic of Byzantium was the use of the cupola and vaulting on a square ground plan. The cupola was used in the East, Persia and Mesopotamia, where timber was scarce and bricks the usual medium for building. It was placed on a square

by means of a vaulted niche or squinch. The Byzantines employed
this construction, but they also invented their own particular device
for placing a dome on a square. This was the pendentive, or curved
surface, in each of the four angles of the square. The cupolas and
vaulting gave the building the appearance of a Greek cross (i.e. a
cross with equal arms) from the outside, though the ground plan
was a square. Hence this type of building is called a 'cross-in-
square'. At the east end the main apse was flanked on either side by
two smaller ones, and the two little rooms thus formed were called
the diaconicon (sacristy) and the prothesis (used during the early
part of the communion service); at the west end there was usually
a narthex, but no atrium. The exterior of a Byzantine church had
none of the profuse decoration of sculptured figures and ornaments
found in the West. It was often of brick, bare and austere, with
small windows: sometimes ornamentation was provided by patterned brick, as may be seen for instance in churches surviving in
South Italy or in Northern Greece. Occasionally exteriors were
decorated with frescoes, as are certain churches in and near Castoria,
but adornment of this kind was normally reserved for the interior
where it had a special significance.

Figures in sculpture were rarely found and after the iconoclast
controversy were apparently not used for monumental works. The
eastern tradition of carving in low relief was inherited from the
Roman Empire where it had long been used for many purposes, as
for example the portrayal of narrative on a triumphal column or
arch. Carved figures and motifs combining Hellenistic and Eastern
elements appear in both secular and Christian art in the Byzantine
Empire. They were found on coffins (sarcophagi) and ivories.
Carving was freely used for interior ecclesiastical decoration on
pillars or on the pulpit, on the screens across the sanctuary or the
parapet of the gallery. The capitals of the columns show how this
kind of decoration tended to become flat rather than raised; for
instance the acanthus motif no longer stood out, but was more in
the nature of a decorative design. The 'champlevé' technique of
making hollows in the marble and filling it with a dark contrasting
substance was employed, as at Daphni or Mistra. Something of this
kind can also be seen in the cloister next door to the cathedral of
Monreale, where graceful columns inlaid with mosaic work are
found side by side with others adorned with sculptured scenes.

The greatest heights of Byzantine art are reached in interior
decoration where the medium employed was either mosaic or fresco.
Mosaic artists used small cubes of glass or marble to portray scenes

and figures, usually against a gold background. These cubes, which were inserted into a plaster foundation, varied in size according to the effect desired. They are found in almost every nuance, and in different materials, including enamel and gold and silver. This method was specially suited to the curved surfaces of Byzantine architecture, and the artists and craftsmen knew how to get exactly the right effect when the mosaic was viewed from a distance by the worshipper in the body of the church. Something of the range of colour and shape and the craftsmanship can be perceived from the detailed reproductions which have been made of certain mosaics, for instance of the panels of Justinian and Theodora in San Vitale in Ravenna,[1] or from the eleventh- and twelfth-century imperial panels found in Hagia Sophia in Constantinople.[2] But the effect which the artist intended can only been seen by standing in the church and viewing the mosaics in different lights, or when the candles are lit for a service. The other method of mural decoration was fresco (paint applied to a surface of plaster). This was not so expensive as mosaic and was widely employed in the later middle ages when the Empire was reduced in wealth and territory. It is also found earlier, as in the vigorous, if crude, popular art in the churches of Cappadocia in Asia Minor. In Rome examples dating from different periods have survived, showing both Latin and Greek styles of painting (e.g. in the lower church of San Clemente, or in S. Maria Antiqua in the *forum romanum*).

In the Byzantine Empire comparatively little remains from the seventh to the tenth century. This is partly because of the Muslim invasions, and more particularly because of the iconoclast controversy in the eighth and ninth centuries. The ban on any representation of the human figure in the Church had been accompanied by destruction or mutilation of ecclesiastical art which infringed this ruling. With the triumph of icon veneration and the end of major theological controversies Byzantium launched into a period of victorious expansion, both material and cultural. Art was no exception. The evolution of the new iconography is hinted at in literary sources, as the description of Basil I's buildings. The monuments belonging to this Macedonian period no longer exist, but the mosaic decoration which was one of the major achievements of Byzantine art can be seen at its finest in churches of the eleventh century,

1. See A. Grabar, *Byzantine Painting* (Skira series), or the relevant Batsford *Iris Colour Books*.
2. T. Whittemore, *The Mosaics of Haghia Sophia at Istanbul*, vol. III (O.U.P. 1942).

particularly Hosios Lukas and Daphni in Greece and Nea Moni on
the island of Chios. Artists and craftsmen followed the accepted
scheme of iconography. Its aim was primarily theological: it was
concerned with the dogma of the Trinity and the redemption of the
world by God the Son. Particular figures and scenes had their special
place in the church: Christ the All-Powerful occupied the cupola;
the Virgin was in the apse; on the vaulting before the apse was an
empty throne, 'the prepared throne' of Revelation (the Hetimasia),
containing the instruments of Christ's passion, thus symbolising his
first and second comings; in the sanctuary the liturgy was shown
being celebrated by Christ and the angels; in the nave were the great
church festivals, as the Nativity, the Crucifixion, the Dormition (the
death, or 'falling asleep') of the Virgin; the narthex had scenes from
the life of the Virgin; the rest of the space of walls and vaulting was
filled with figures of apostles, martyrs, prophets, saints, arranged
hierarchically. There were certain variations, sometimes dictated by
local needs. The warrior saints were displayed in a prominent
position in disputed frontier districts; the two St Theodores and St
Demetrius still stand out in frescoes surviving in Macedonian
churches. The tenth-century St Luke Stiriotes understandably
occupies a relatively important place in the church of the monastery
in the mountains above his village of Stiris in Phocis.

The interior of a Byzantine church thus reflected the universe, the
cosmos, with the cupola as heaven, the place of honour containing
the Pantocrator, the middle zone as paradise and the lowest zone as
earth. The technique of the mosaic artists was superb: by their
perspective and their command of their materials and their use of
curved surfaces they so created the figures of the heavenly hierarchy
that the worshippers in the church below could feel that these were
actually present. 'In Byzantium, the beholder was not kept at a
distance from the image; he entered within its aura of sanctity, and
the image, in turn, partook of the space in which he moved.'[1]

In iconography this plan varied little, but there was considerable
difference of style and execution. The Crucifixion scene of Daphni
(c. 1100) with its restraint and dignity looks almost like sculpture in
colour and reflects a classical influence. The centurion from the
Crucifixion of Chios (c. 1050) is a vigorous gesticulating 'oriental'
figure in vivid colours far more in the tradition of the popular art
found in some of the illustrations to monastic works. Generally
speaking, it was the humanist trend of Daphni which prevailed in

1. Otto Demus, *Byzantine Mosaic Decoration*, p. 4, to whom I am greatly
indebted.

the twelfth century. Some of the finest achievements in both mosaics and frescoes were outside Byzantine territory in the Norman kingdom of Sicily and in the Balkans. The full flowering of Byzantine art is seen in the frescoes of the Macedonian church of Nereži (1164), now a predominantly Muslim village about four miles from Skopje. Its Pietà is unsurpassed of its kind.

The expansion of Byzantine art from the end of the ninth century down to the capture of the city in 1204 is seen not only in its monumental work but in small objects, often executed for connoisseurs at home or abroad, such as illustrated books or ivory jewel caskets or enamel work or textiles.

The printing presses of Byzantium were the *scriptoria* where manuscripts were copied by hand. Amongst the older manuscripts are the 'purple' codices whose dates range from the end of the fifth to the sixth century; these contain parts of the Bible written in silver on purple vellum. Manuscripts with elaborate and carefully executed illustrations would probably be commissioned by some princely or wealthy patron. Often not only the text, but the illustrations, were reproduced. Thus the ninth-century copy of the travels of Cosmas Indicopleustes repeats the miniatures of the original manuscript (which Cosmas himself did), and there are ninth- or tenth-century copies of parts of the Old and New Testaments or the Psalter which obviously belong to a 'family', stemming from a much older original. These illustrations are in various styles. Some, the Paris Psalter for instance, have Alexandrian characteristics, seen in the landscape background, the personification of abstract qualities and an allegorical element. Others show oriental leanings in their rich colour and intricate decorative motifs. Certain illuminated manuscripts do not belong at all to these aristocratic luxury products. They are illustrated in a racy, even satirical, style and were for more popular consumption. Political or religious opponents are mercilessly pilloried—for instance in a Psalter perhaps produced in the stronghold of the iconophiles, the Studite monastery in Constantinople, the iconoclasts are shown crucifying Christ. Amazing scenes from everyday life and streaks of originality crop up from time to time in miniatures of a similar kind, such as the unusual iconography and colour of the monk James of Kokkinobaphus' illustration to the sermons on the Virgin, or the lively little cartoons (almost after the style of the English *Punch*) in the Madrid manuscript of Scylitzes' history.

The tradition and resources of Byzantium at the height of its power were equally displayed in other works of art. The Byzantines had mastered the technique of cloisonné work, and their enamels are in a class by themselves. Some of the finest are preserved in St Mark's, Venice. Goldsmiths' work, such as has survived, was of an equally high quality. Small-scale sculpture in ivory was evidently not regarded as suspect. Ivories fall into two groups: religious and secular.[1] The former might be triptychs or reliquaries with religious subjects carved on them. Secular ivories were often luxury objects, such as jewel-boxes, and they were decorated with stories from mythology or scenes from hunting and other everyday pursuits. The Byzantine genius for design and colour was reflected in the quality of its textiles. These were used in church as vestments and as hangings. Paul the Silentiary eloquently described the beauty of the ciborium curtains in Hagia Sophia. Such materials would be part of the normal furnishings of the imperial court or of wealthy private families. They found a ready market abroad and their designs carried the various motifs of Byzantine art into different parts of the civilised world.

With the gradual disintegration of the Empire following the capture of Constantinople in 1204 Byzantine economy was seriously affected. This had repercussions on art. Small works of art, as the expensive illuminated manuscripts, became rare. Fresco, and not the more costly mosaic, was generally used in churches. But all the same, art, like literary activities, continued to flourish, and twelfth-century developments run on into the period after 1204. The most lively centres in the later middle ages were in comparative outposts, as Mistra in the Peloponnese, or Trebizond, and in other countries of the Orthodox persuasion, notably the Balkans and Russia. The finest works of this period were the religious wall paintings, particularly in the Balkans in the twelfth and thirteenth centuries. Different churches show distinct individuality, but in general there was a movement away from the more abstract eleventh-century art, to a more humanist interpretation. Though certain features of the middle Byzantine iconographical scheme are retained, by the fourteenth century the walls tend to become overloaded with scenes (as for instance in St Clement of Ochrida). Whatever the elegance and originality of the thirteenth-century Serbian Sopočani or Mileševo, or the Chora Monastery (Kariye Djamii) in Constantinople, this promise, unlike that of the contemporary West, remained unfulfilled. Perhaps the arrest was to some extent due to Orthodox conservatism which historical events had strengthened; it was certainly also one of the results of the Ottoman conquest.

1. Some of these can be seen in London in the Victoria and Albert Museum.

XI

BYZANTIUM AND ITS NEIGHBOURS

Geography alone was sufficient to determine that Byzantium must daily meet those whose ways of life and modes of thought were not its own. Its problems and its opportunities differed in East, North and West.

With the East contact was traditional, and respect (in the middle ages at any rate) mutual. The Graeco-Roman world and the world of the Middle East upheld recognised, if rival, civilisations. Islam borrowed freely from the way of life found in conquered Byzantine provinces, or from the resources of Greek scholarship which lay at its doors. And the Byzantines did likewise. One particularly noticeable instance of this cross-fertilisation is found in Byzantine monasticism and in its *Vitae sanctorum*. Non-Hellenic elements were frequently introduced into Byzantine hagiology and hagiography, and there was constant interchange of ideas owing to factors such as polyglot monastic centres, oriental colonies within the Christian world, as in Jerusalem or Constantinople or Mt Athos, and the existence of frontier districts (for instance in Georgia or Armenia) where different churches exercised what can be best described as a condominium.

In the North, that is in the Balkans, beyond the Danube and in the Black Sea area, contacts were inevitable from the start and relations on an entirely different footing. The migratory Slavonic and Hunnic tribes were a constant menace. And it is here in the North that some of the greatest and more obvious work of Byzantium was achieved, and large numbers of the barbarian invaders were assimilated, particularly in the Balkan and Greek themes, though scholars are still arguing as to precisely how much Slavonic blood was absorbed into the population of the Peloponnese in the early middle ages. On the other hand, there were many tribes who could neither be kept out of the Balkans nor absorbed into the provinces of the Empire, and these were able to grow to maturity and develop their own principalities during the middle ages under the tutelage of Constantinople, as for instance Serbia or Bulgaria.

In the Christian West the situation was different and changed greatly in the course of the middle ages. Whatever claims to universal empire Constantinople made, from the fifth century to the eleventh century it had fewer direct contacts with the West than with the North or East. There was in the early middle ages no civilisation in the West comparable with that of Byzantium or Islam; it was a less populated area and more primitive. Italy of course was the half-way house and was partly in Byzantine hands, and it was as much over concrete claims in Italy and the Adriatic as over the imperial question that Constantinople and the Carolingians clashed. But the situation was radically altered by the expansion and development of the West, and more particularly by the eleventh-century Norman conquest of Sicily and South Italy, by the western crusading enterprises sponsored by a revitalised and powerful Papacy, and by the growth of civic life in Italy with increasingly vigorous economic activities. At a time when it looked as though Slavonic and other migratory movements were being stabilised in the Balkans, Constantinople found herself caught between Turk and Latin in a pincer movement from East and West. The growth of the nation and city-state in the West, the Moscovite kingdom in the North, the Ottoman emirate in Asia Minor, the Slavonic kingdoms in the Balkans, introduced into later Byzantine diplomacy an intricacy unparalleled in its early history.

It is against this background of frontier problems and diplomatic change that the influence of the Byzantine polity must be considered. And it is understandable that the greater debt was owed by the less developed groups in more immediate contact with Constantinople, and their outlook was to some extent determined by that of their near neighbour. Whatever the interpretation, and however much the structure of society developed on essentially native lines, it is difficult to deny that the young states which took shape during the middle ages, such as Serbia or Bosnia or Bulgaria (this last was from the eleventh to the end of the twelfth century part of the Byzantine Empire) or Kievan, and later Muscovite, Russia, borrowed much from their experienced neighbour, particularly in statecraft and administration.

Above all, the Orthodox Church, apart from what it had to give in its own right, was an exponent of the Byzantine way of life. The Christian year with its round of festivals and fasts was related not only to the needs of each individual, but was regarded as the outward manifestation of the inner significance of the Christian Empire. When God condescended to reveal Himself Incarnate in time and space, He sanctified the process of history, and the Christian world could be a reflection, a *mimesis*, on earth of the *civitas caelestis*. In all the church services of the liturgical year the Emperor and his officials, together with the Patriarch and the clergy, had their appointed places. The words of responses and acclamations proper to the season show what supreme importance was attached to the imperial function. It was this conception of the Christian State, with the close inter-dependence of priest and ruler, which deeply impressed the Slav peoples and was reflected in their own medieval life. It was true that Byzantium only envisaged one supreme Emperor, but under him could be many lesser lights, and in time it was to a Slav kingdom that the imperial Roman and Christian responsibilities were handed on when Constantinople was occupied by the Turks in 1453 and a Byzantine Palaeologan princess, Sophia Palaeologina, married the Muscovite Ivan.

It was not only in countries where the Orthodox Church had taken root that the Byzantine interpretation of the Roman imperial tradition was a factor of significance. In the early middle ages the New Rome, Constantinople, kept alive for Western, as well as Eastern, Christendom the conception of Empire, and to the Christian this could only be thought of in terms of a Roman Empire as refashioned by Constantine the Great. Medieval political developments in what had once been the *pars occidentalis* did not favour any reconstruction of a Constantinian world, nor yet that imitation of the *Romaioi* of Constantinople which is found in Slav principalities. Western rulers did nevertheless revive for their own benefit what was at first under Charles the Great little more than the title of 'Emperor' but which from the days of the Ottonian emperors came to be associated with certain rights over territory in Italy, Burgundy and Germany. This emergence in the Latin world of a western empire, the Holy Roman Empire as it came to be called, has been in recent years the subject of controversy. But there is no doubt about the existence of an initial Latin debt to the East, or the way in which a variety of contacts between Byzantium and the West helped to fill out and stimulate the western interpretation of the imperial office.

Both Latin and Slavonic countries also inherited, though in varying degree, Roman legal principles as interpreted by the Byzantines. The transmission of Justinian's legal work or of the later medieval East Roman Codes was a basic and fundamental service performed by a highly organised Empire, and, in different ways, countries of Europe and the Mediterranean world drew on such resources and experience. The *Corpus Juris Civilis* of Justinian and its reception in the West is well known, but less publicity has been given to the collections issued by the later Byzantine rulers, such as the *Basilica*, partly because less work has been done on them. The Slav peoples drew extensively on Byzantine legal collections, parts of which they had in translation. Less to be expected, perhaps, is the evidence which points to the continued usage of Byzantine law in South Italy. The Calabrian manual of rural and urban laws, which was compiled in Basil II's reign from the *Ecloga* of Leo III and the *Procheiros Nomos* of Basil I, was being used by the Norman princes of the twelfth century and was revised in Roger II's day. An examination of the various legal handbooks in use not only in the Balkans, but further afield, as in South Italy, or in Palestine and Syria, reveals either (as in the Balkans) deliberate building with the help of Byzantine theory and practice, or (as in South Italy) the continued usage and adaptation of what had long been part of the law of the countryside.

It was also possible to learn something of the principles of Byzantine government in many other ways. This is evident from the two books compiled in the middle of the tenth century by the humanist Emperor Constantine VII. The *De Cerimoniis* regulated the externals of daily life in Byzantine imperial circles and provided a model for other courts and princes. The *De Administrando Imperio* taught the young Caesar his imperial craft, and it explains to us, no less than to him, the principles of Byzantine foreign policy. The information obtained from the foreign office, from various administrative departments, from diplomats and provincial governors, not only demonstrates Byzantine method, but shows some of the means and channels whereby knowledge of Byzantine civilisation and government penetrated into other countries.

There were many informal links between the far West and Constantinople, particularly from the eleventh century onwards. Before 1204, England had come into contact with Byzantium through the recruitment of the imperial bodyguard and through ties of marriage. There are contemporary references to the famous 'axe-bearing warriors' of the Varangian Guard, not always complimentary, as when the Abbot of Patmos in 1088 petitioned against the billeting of troops amongst whom 'those English soldiers' are mentioned. Byzantine acceptance of this source of recruitment is reflected in the late twelfth-century John Cinnamus' *History* where he speaks of 'the British race who have long served the Roman Emperors', and appreciation of their quality is shown when an Emperor of the same century, Manuel Comnenus, sent a cordial letter to the English Henry II which Roger of Hoveden quotes. After the defeat of the Byzantines by the Turks in Asia Minor in 1176, Manuel wrote, 'We have felt it a pleasure that it so happened that some of the chief men of your nobility were with us . . . and we thought we should like to inform you as being our dearly beloved friend and as being so closely united with our imperial majesty by the ties of blood.' Manuel's second wife was from a western crusading family, Mary of Antioch, the daughter of Raymond of Poitiers, uncle of Eleanor of Aquitaine, Henry II's wife, so that Henry's children and Manuel's were cousins. Henry II's accounts also reflect the friendly interest between the two families; the Pipe Rolls have various entries for hospitality to the ambassadors of the Emperor of Constantinople, and items such as the bills for sending a pack of English hounds to Manuel who was a keen huntsman. Courteous gestures of this kind were usual in any period, but in the warm acknowledgement of the ties of blood the later twelfth century has moved far from the exclusive tenth-century policy laid down in the handbook on administration in the matter of imperial marriages. Though it never deviated from the traditional theory of universal supremacy, political circumstances had forced the Byzantine world to modify its attitude towards the 'barbarians'.

In one respect however the Latin and Greek worlds drew apart, not nearer. In religious matters there was not the same attitude as there was in diplomatic intercourse, or administrative usage. The widening rift between Christian and Christian was partly because of intense religious conviction on both sides. But still more important were the political issues which affected ecclesiastical policy. In the earlier middle ages theological or disciplinary differences were raised between Greek and Latin churches, but the determining factor was often Rome's interest in certain relatively unexplored fields of missionary activity, or her demands for the restoration of the ecclesiastical jurisdiction in South Italy and Illyricum of which she had been deprived when this was transferred to the Patriarch of Constantinople in 732. And after 1204 in the later middle ages negotiations for reunion between the Churches were poisoned from the outset by Byzantine popular hatred of the Latin despoilers of the Eastern Empire.

But there is a more positive side to the relations between the Greek Orthodox Church and its neighbours. In its main features this has long been recognised, though details are still being added to our knowledge. In its missionary work Constantinople served a wide area—the East, Russia, the Balkans, and central Europe. It has been suggested that the ninth-century work of the Byzantine missionaries Cyril and Methodius in Moravia was by no means as ephemeral as is sometimes supposed.[1] There is some reason to believe that Slavo-Byzantine culture, including the Slavonic liturgy, held its own for almost two centuries (the tenth and eleventh), and traces of the Eastern rite were found in Bohemia much later. Equally interesting, and pointing in the same direction, are the results of Hungarian research on the Byzantine origin of their own Church.[2] The intensive missionary work of the Eastern Church among the Turkish and Hunnic tribes in the early middle ages, especially from the sixth century onwards, has been emphasised; such activities, as well as contacts with converted Slavs, introduced the Magyars to Christianity before they reached Hungary, and when they got there they found both Rome and Byzantium at work. Moreover in spite of King Stephen's decision in favour of the West there is evidence for the continuity of Greek influence on Hungarian soil. This was not surprising in view of Hungary's political and family links with Constantinople. In the eleventh and twelfth centuries certain Greek monasteries were founded in Hungary, and except for a brief period in the thirteenth century they were under the control of the Patriarch of Constantinople. There are in Hungary legends and sagas of Byzantine origin, place names connected with Byzantine saints and in the early twelfth century translations were made of John of Damascus' *De Fide Orthodoxa* and Maximus the Confessor's writings.

The missionary work of Constantinople was followed by administrative consolidation and the establishment of ecclesiastical institutions. In Hungary and Moravia, and South Italy (where Byzantium was not of course called upon to initiate pioneer work), this was shared with, and finally for the most part surrendered to, the Latin Church. In other regions converted by Constantinople the Christian life was lived after the Orthodox form. The secular church, with its parishes, dioceses and provinces under its metropolitan, was ultimately subordinated to the Patriarch of Constantinople. The

1. Cf. *Dumbarton Oaks Papers* XIX (1965), where there are papers on various aspects of the Byzantine mission to the Slavs by G. Ostrogorsky, G. C. Soulis, D. Obolensky and A. Dostál.
2. See especially the work of G. Moravcsik and M. Gyóni.

upper hierarchy of the secular clergy were sometimes appointed from among the Byzantine clergy, particularly in Russia and the Balkans. Monastic life in both the cenobitic and eremitic tradition was as enthusiastically developed as on Byzantine soil. In the monastic world, the humblest monk might live a cosmopolitan life. Monks from Mt Athos are found in Poland or Russia and in the eastern houses, and pilgrimage was almost an obligation. Athos was inhabited and visited by men from all parts of the Christian world. Not only experience of living practice in the older centres, but translations of the Greek monastic classics brought to the more remote and younger members of the Orthodox Church knowledge of early and medieval Greek and eastern monastic traditions. The life of the early fourth-century Egyptian Antony, or accounts of the seventh-century Judaean settlements in the time of Cyril of Scytho-polis, were read in Old Slavonic versions in the monastic houses of Bulgaria or of Kievan Russia. Thus St Basil and St Theodore the Studite were by no means the only, or perhaps the most important, influences in medieval Orthodox monasticism.

The care and wisdom of the Orthodox Church in providing the liturgical framework of daily worship (though not necessarily in the Greek language) and in giving access to the fundamental works of the great theologians and the spiritual leaders of the Christian Church need in general no comment. But Byzantium gave too the music which was an integral part of public worship, whether in parish or monastic chapel. Byzantine music influenced developments in Bulgaria, which in the ninth century got both services and chants from Constantinople and transmitted these to the Russians in the tenth century.[1]

Art and architecture are subjects too wide to be treated here, but it is possible just to indicate the lines on which scholars are working. Exacting canons of criticism are being applied to regional art and architecture, as well as to motifs and works of art which by their nature may be described as 'travellers'—manuscripts, coins, carved ivories, or the kind of material found in England in the Sutton Hoo burial ship. Otto Demus in a series of brilliant studies is analysing the iconography and appraising the technique of mosaic work in Greece, Italy and Sicily, showing Venetian and Sicilian indebtedness to the iconography of Byzantine liturgical tradition and to the trained craftsmen who executed this work, and whose masterpieces can still be seen at Daphni or Hosios Lukas or Cephalù.

1. The relevant manuscripts are written in the oldest form of the Slavonic, i.e. old Bulgarian which had adopted Byzantine musical notation.

Art forms are by their nature more cosmopolitan than a literary medium. The writings of the Byzantines were generally available only in areas where Greek was still used, or through a translation. But it must again be remembered that we have only just begun systematic exploration of the extent to which Byzantine literature and philosophy, science and the occult studies, entered into the cultural and popular life of the neighbouring world. In some cases, particularly philosophy and science, as yet very little is known even about the tradition and development within the Empire. But the fundamental gift to East and West alike of Aristotelian logic and the notion of conceptual thought should be emphasised. To John of Damascus it seemed proper to begin his book on the Christian faith with a section on logic; that was part of his Hellenic background, not forgotten even though he lived in a Muslim world. And Aristotelian concepts, this conceptual framework, though not natural to some eastern modes of thought, did also influence medieval Islam. At the other end of the scale there was a host of popular and even trivial customs which travelled to Slavonic countries and even on occasion as far afield as England—stories and ballads, oracles and charms, incantations against minor ills, as insomnia, nose-bleedings and headaches.

Paradoxically enough it was only after 1204, when the Latins took forcible possession of parts of the Byzantine Empire and when the gulf between the Greek and Latin Churches seemed to become really unbridgeable, that eastern and western Christians got to know each other's literature. The diversion of the Fourth Crusade to capture a Christian Empire has met with well-deserved condemnation. But in some ways it undeniably brought East and West together in a happier sense. Latin families intermarried with the Byzantines; their children were brought up in Greece. The thirteenth-century William of Villehardouin, ruler of the principality of Achaea, was born and lived as a child in his father's castle at Kalamata in the Peloponnese and spoke fluent Greek. The Latin rulers of Greece learnt to know and to appreciate its glories. Once more its monuments became famous in the outside world: King Pedro IV of Aragon wrote in 1380 that the Acropolis, the Castell de Cetines as it was called in Catalan documents, was 'the richest jewel in all the world, the like of which no other king in Christendom could match'.[1] Personal experience in the Aegean brought not only appreciation of Greek

1. Quoted by K. M. Setton, *Catalan domination of Athens 1311–1388* (Cambridge, Mass. 1948), p. 187. 'Cetines' was a Latin corruption of the demotic phrase for 'Athens', the locative 'eis Athenas'.

and Byzantine art, but knowledge of the literary and intellectual traditions of the two worlds. We are constantly made aware of these cross-currents—Byzantines devouring St Augustine or St Thomas Aquinas in translation, Latins reading Homer also in translation, both to some extent learning to understand the other, in contrast to the eleventh century when Psellus did not seem to know the difference between Caesar and Cicero.

There were unending opportunities for contact between Byzantium and its neighbours and they lent and borrowed freely. The influence of Byzantium was both direct and indirect. Its services in handing on to the modern world some of the writings of ancient Greece are well known. Of equal significance for Christian civilisation was the leading part taken by Greek-speaking theologians during the formative period of the fourth to the seventh centuries and largely made available to the West through translations. This was a specifically 'Greek' contribution: it had its roots in the Hellenic capacity for articulate thought, and it was made within the framework of the East Roman Empire, which was the medieval Greek Empire. Greek culture in the middle ages was built on classical Greek life, but it was something living and organic, capable of expressing itself in the idiom of its own day.

(style)

LIST OF LATE ROMAN AND BYZANTINE RULERS

(For a more complete list and genealogical tables see G. Ostrogorsky, *History of the Byzantine State*. With few exceptions, only names mentioned in the text are given here. Rulers not belonging to the dynasty under which they appear, though they were often united to it by marriage, are marked thus *.)

285–305	Diocletian
306–337	Constantine I
361–363	Julian the Apostate
379–395	Theodosius I the Great
395–408	Arcadius
395–423	Honorius
408–450	Theodosius II
450–457	Marcian
457–474	Leo I
474–475 and 476–491	Zeno
491–518	Anastasius I
518–527	Justin I
527–565	Justinian I
582–602	Maurice
602–610	Phocas

———————

Heraclian Dynasty

610–641	Heraclius
641–668	Constans II
668–685	Constantine IV
685–695 and 705–711	Justinian II

Syrian or 'Isaurian' Dynasty
- 717–741 Leo III
- 741–775 Constantine V
- 775–780 Leo IV
- 780–797 Constantine VI
- 797–802 Irene (wife of Leo IV)

Amorian Dynasty
- 820–829 Michael II
- 829–842 Theophilus
- 842–867 Michael III

Macedonian Dynasty
- 867– 886 Basil I
- 886– 912 Leo VI the Wise
- 913– 959 Constantine VII Porphyrogenitus
- 920– 944 *Romanus I Lecapenus
- 959– 963 Romanus II
- 963– 969 *Nicephorus II Phocas
- 969– 976 *John I Tzimisces
- 976–1025 Basil II
- 1025–1028 Constantine VIII
- 1028–1050 Zoe, married

(1) *Romanus III	1028–1034
(2) *Michael IV	1034–1041
adopted *Michael V	1041–1042
(3) *Constantine IX Monomachus	1042–1055

1042 and 1055–1056 Theodora, sister of Zoe

- 1057–1059 Isaac I Comnenus
- 1059–1067 Constantine X Ducas
- 1068–1071 Romanus IV Diogenes
- 1071–1078 Michael VII Ducas
- 1078–1081 Nicephorus III Botaneiates

Comnenian Dynasty
- 1081–1118 Alexius I Comnenus
- 1118–1143 John II Comnenus
- 1143–1180 Manuel I Comnenus
- 1180–1183 Alexius II Comnenus
- 1183–1185 Andronicus I Comnenus

Dynasty of the Angeli
   1185–1195   Isaac II Angelus
   1195–1203   Alexius III Angelus
   1203–1204   Isaac II (again) and Alexius IV Angeli
   1204   *Alexius V Murtzuphlus

Dynasty of the Lascarids
   1204–1222   Theodore I Lascaris
   1222–1254   *John III Ducas Vatatzes
   1254–1258   Theodore II Lascaris
   1258–1259   John IV Lascaris

Dynasty of the Palaeologi
   1259–1282   Michael VIII
   1282–1328   Andronicus II
   1328–1341   Andronicus III
   1341–1391   John V
   1347–1354   *John VI Cantacuzenus
   1391–1425   Manuel II
   1425–1448   John VIII
   1449–1453   Constantine XI

Note: Byzantine chronology often presents complicated problems and scholars sometimes differ in their dating. Here I have followed G. Ostrogorsky, *History of the Byzantine State*.

BIBLIOGRAPHICAL NOTES

(Most of the books cited contain further bibliography.)

GENERAL

A masterly survey with excellent bibliographies and discussion of original sources is provided by G. Ostrogorsky, *History of the Byzantine State* (Blackwell, Oxford 1968; this is the second English edition based on the 3rd German ed., Munich 1963, with some bibliographical additions). A readable but rather more discursive treatment is given in A. A. Vasiliev, *History of the Byzantine Empire* (Madison 1952). A brilliant introduction to Byzantium is to be found in two essays by N. H. Baynes, 'The Hellenistic Civilisation and East Rome' (O.U.P. 1946) and 'The Thought-World of East Rome' (O.U.P. 1947) reprinted in *Byzantine Studies and Other Essays* (London 1955). There is an excellent short survey of the early period from the third century A.D. to the death of Justinian by G. Downey, *The Late Roman Empire* (New York 1969). N. H. Baynes, *The Byzantine Empire* (London 1925), gives a short study which within its self-imposed limits is a classic, *Byzantium*, edited by N. H. Baynes and H. St L. B. Moss (Oxford 1948), contains essays on different aspects of Byzantine history by experts in their own fields (particularly valuable are the contributions by N. H. Baynes, W. Ensslin, R. M. Dawkins and H. Grégoire). L. Bréhier, *Le Monde Byzantin* (3 vols. Paris 1947–50), covers most aspects of Byzantine history and life. C. Diehl, *Byzantium: Greatness and Decline* (New Brunswick 1957), is a translation of a stimulating essay, *Byzance, grandeur et décadence,* originally published in 1919; P. Charanis adds a valuable bibliographical note and introduction. In his *Byzantine Portraits* (New York 1927) C. Diehl gives lively sketches of well-known Byzantine characters. An excellent general introduction to the years 610–1071 is to be found in R. J. H. Jenkins, *Byzantium: the Imperial Centuries* (London 1966). The *Cambridge Medieval History*, vol. IV, *The Eastern Roman Empire 717–1453* (1923), has now been replaced by a new vol. IV in two parts, *The Byzantine Empire 717–1453*, pt. I, *Byzantium and her Neighbours* (1966) and pt. II, *Government, Church and Civilisation* (1967); introductory surveys, and certain topics, such as Art and Architecture, go back to the fourth century. On administration with special reference to the navy see H. Ahrweiler, *Byzance et la mer: la marine de guerre, la politique et les institutions maritimes de Byzance aux VIIe–XVe siècles* (Paris 1966). Among studies on special topics a distinguished contribution is that of F. Dvornik, *The Photian Schism* (C.U.P. 1948), which throws new light on the career of the Patriarch Photius and particularly on his relations with the Papacy, and explains how the legend of Photius as an arch-heretic arose in Latin circles. The rôle of Byzantium during the crusading period has now been reassessed. S. Runciman, *A History of the Crusades*, 3 vols. (C.U.P. 1951–4) gives a graphic narrative account. A longer *History of the Crusades* (gen. ed. K. M. Setton) is planned in five volumes of which so far I (1955) and II (1962) have appeared, covering the period to 1311. In this work a team of experts give their views on various aspects of the crusading movement; there are particularly valuable contributions from the orientalists, including H. A. R. Gibb, B. Lewis, C. Cahen and S. Der Nersessian. C. M. Brand provides a general survey of Byzantium during the period of the Third and Fourth Crusades in *Byzantium confronts the West 1180–1204* (Cambridge: Mass. 1968). The *Dumbarton Oaks Papers,* which now appear every year, are always well worth consulting; they contain studies on most aspects of Byzantine civilisation and history.

THE CHURCH AND MONASTIC LIFE

R. M. French, *The Eastern Orthodox Church* (London 1951), gives a sound but very brief survey which deals with the Church to the present day, thus bringing out the continuity in its life. A good deal of value is given incidentally in P. Hammond, *The Waters of Marah: the Present State of the Greek Church* (London 1956). Based on the personal experiences of an English scholar in Greece in the difficult days after the war, this provides one of the best introductions to a study of the Greek Church. N. Zernov gives a lively account of the Greek Church (though with some inaccuracies) in *Eastern Christendom* (London 1961). A good bird's-eye view may be found in T. Ware, *The Orthodox Church* (Pelican 1963).

Relations with the Papacy to 1204 are covered by S. Runciman, *The Eastern Schism* (Oxford 1956), and for the later middle ages are admirably discussed by J. Gill, *The Council of Florence* (C.U.P. 1959). G. Every, *The Byzantine Patriarchate 451–1204* (2nd ed., London 1962), is stimulating but somewhat given to speculation.

E. Wellesz, *A History of Byzantine Music and Hymnography* (2nd ed., Oxford 1961), is an excellent account of an important aspect of Byzantine civilisation by a master of the subject who has done much to decipher its musical notation.

S. Salaville, *An Introduction to the Study of Eastern Liturgies* (translated by J. M. T. Barton, London 1938).

There is no full general account of Byzantine monasticism in English or French known to me. For those who read Latin there is a good constitutional survey in P. de Meester, *De Monachico Statu Iuxta Disciplinam Byzantinam* (Vatican 1942). See also the *Cambridge Medieval History* IV, pt. II, ch. 26.

For an excellent account of early monasticism see D. J. Chitty, *The Desert a City* (Blackwell, Oxford 1966). E. Amand de Mendieta, *La presqu'île des caloyers: le Mont-Athos* (Bruges 1955), gives a lively picture of present-day Mt Athos interpolated with various scholarly digressions on its past history. C. Cavarnos, *Anchored in God* (Athens 1959), gives an excellent brief account of contemporary conditions. D. M. Nicol provides a good history of the houses 'in the air' in his *Meteora: the Rock Monasteries of Thessaly* (London 1963). Much information about individual hermits and monks and monasteries is to be found in the copious lives of the saints; for an English translation of three of these see E. Dawes and N. H. Baynes, *Three Byzantine Saints* (Blackwell, Oxford 1948).

What Byzantines thought about their Church, and the nature of their spiritual life, is best revealed by their own writings and by the rulings of the Church Councils. Some of these may be found in translation: e.g. St Basil, *Ascetical Works*, trans. M. M. Wagner (New York 1950) or trans. W. Lowther Clarke (London 1925); *Nicene and Post-Nicene Fathers of the Christian Church*, vol. IX, St John of Damascus, *Exposition of the Orthodox Faith* (London 1899), and vol. XIV, *The Seven Ecumenical Councils of the Undivided Church* (London 1900); and *Early Fathers from the Philokalia* and *Writings from the Philokalia*, trans E. Kadloubovsky and G. E. H. Palmer (London 1954), both of which are based on the Slav translations of the Greek original and need to be used with caution. The *Sources Chrétiennes* series provides French translations of the writings of Byzantine monks and churchmen (e.g. Maximus the Confessor and above all Symeon the New Theologian). Nicholas Cabasilas, *The Divine Liturgy*, is translated by J. M. Hussey and P. A. McNulty (S.P.C.K. 1960). An introductory survey is given by V. Lossky, *The Mystical Theology of the Eastern Church* (London 1957), and more briefly in *Orthodox Spirituality* by a Monk of the Eastern Church (S.P.C.K. 1945). There are some excellent general articles by Archbishop Basil Krivocheine on Byzantine monasticism and spirituality, e.g. 'Mt Athos in the Spiritual Life of the Orthodox Church', *The Christian East*, New Series, vol. II, no. 2 (autumn 1952), and 'The Brother-Loving Poor Man', *ibid.*, nos. 7 and 8 (winter 1953–4).

See also the chapters on ecclesiastical organisation and monasticism in J. M. Hussey, *Church and Learning in the Byzantine Empire 867–1185* (O.U.P. repr. 1963) and the relevant vols. (by various authors of the *Histoire de l'Église*, ed. A. Fliche and V. Martin. The new *Cambridge Medieval History* IV, pt. II has chapters (with bibliography) on the Secular Church (E. Herman), Liturgy and Music (E. Wellesz), Monasticism and Spirituality (J. M. Hussey). The French ecclesiastical dictionaries (at present in progress) are invaluable works of reference (e.g. *Dict. de droit canonique, Dict. de théol. cath., Dict. d'hist. et de géogr. ecclés, Dict. de spiritualité*).

SOCIAL AND ECONOMIC AND EVERYDAY LIFE

There is nothing that could be described as a satisfactory comprehensive history, though there are some first-rate general chapters in S. Runciman, *Byzantine Civilisation* (London 1933), notably 'Town and Country Life'. A stimulating discussion on certain developments in Byzantium is to be found in H. W. Haussig, *Kulturgeschichte von Byzanz*, 2nd ed. (Stuttgart 1966; an English translation, *A History of Byzantine Civilisation*, Thames and Hudson, is in the press). A vivid picture of life in the capital in the early period is given by G. Downey, *Constantinople in the Age of Justinian* (Oklahoma 1960).

On the economic side the *Cambridge Economic History*, vol. I (2nd ed., 1966) contains a chapter by G. Ostrogorsky on agrarian conditions and vol. II (1952) a chapter on trade by S. Runciman. The complex and controversial problems of economic conditions and the question of 'feudalism' continue to be examined, particularly by Russian scholars. Recent views on agrarian developments in Byzantium will be found in the detailed studies of scholars such as G. Ostrogorsky or P. Lemerle; see the references in G. Ostrogorsky, *History of the Byzantine State* (Blackwell, Oxford 1968). Two particularly important works in this field are by G. Ostrogorsky, *Pour l'histoire de la féodalité byzantine* (Paris 1954) and *Quelques problèmes d'histoire de la paysannerie byzantine* (Brussels 1956). The *Cambridge Medieval History* IV, pt. II contains a good deal of information *passim*, especially ch. 22 (R. J. H. Jenkins on Social Life) and ch. 28 (K. Vogel on Byzantine Science).

Two lively studies on certain aspects of Byzantine civilisation are E. Jeanselme et L. Œconomos, *Les Œuvres d'Assistance et les Hôpitaux Byzantins au siècle des Comnènes,* Communication faite au Iᵉʳ Congrès de l'Histoire de l'Art de Guèrir, Anvers 1920 (Anvers 1921), and C. Diehl, *La Société Byzantine à l'époque des Comnènes* (Paris 1929). On welfare work there is a full account by D. J. Constantelos, *Byzantine Philanthropy and Social Welfare* (New Brunswick 1968). But the interested reader will probably get most satisfaction from investigating for himself the information to be found in the sources. In addition to translations cited above under 'The Church and Monastic Life', see especially *Rhodian Law, Farmer's Law, Book of the Prefect,* and other legal codes translated by E. H. Freshfield (Cambridge 1927–31); the *Farmer's Law* is also translated by W. Ashburner, *Journal of Hellenic Studies* 32 (1912).

LITERATURE

Besides the translations of sources already referred to, see *Digenes Akrites* trans. J. Mavrogordato (O.U.P. 1956); Michael Psellus, *Chronographia,* trans. E. R. A. Sewter (London 1955 and Penguin 1966 under the title *Fourteen Byzantine Rulers*); Anna Comnena, *Alexiad,* trans. E. A. S. Dawes (London repr. 1967 and as a *Penguin*).

There is no satisfactory full appraisal of Byzantine literature in English known to me. There are two excellent short studies by R. Browning: 'Byzantine Literature' in the *Penguin Companion to Literature*, vol. 4, ed. D. R. Dudley and D. M. Lang (Harmondsworth 1969), pp. 179–215, and 'Byzantine Scholarship' in *Past and Present*, 28 (1964), pp. 3–20. On the linguistic side see R. M. Dawkins in *Byzantium* (ed. N. H. Baynes and H. St L. B. Moss). L. Bréhier gives a general survey in *Le Monde Byzantin*, vol. III, *La Civilisation*; E. Wellesz (*op. cit.*) is excellent for liturgical poetry. See also the introduction to the *Oxford Book of Medieval and Modern Greek Verse*. B. Tatakis provides a short summary in *La Philosophie byzantine* (Paris 1949). There is a survey in the *Cambridge Medieval History* IV, p. II, ch. 27 (F. Dölger on Byzantine Literature).

ART AND ARCHITECTURE

G. Mathew, *Byzantine Aesthetics* (London 1963).

J. A. Hamilton, *Byzantine Architecture and Decoration*, 2nd ed. (London 1956).

T. G. Jackson, *Byzantine and Romanesque Architecture*, 2nd ed., 2 vols (Cambridge 1920).

G. Millet, *L'Ecole grecque dans l'Architecture byzantine* (Paris 1916), is still the standard work on the churches of Greece and their stylistic relations to Constantinople and the other architectural schools of the Empire.

F. M. Simpson, *History of Architectural Development*, vol. II, *Early Christian, Byzantine and Romanesque*. New edition by C. Stewart (London 1954).

On architecture see also the general works cited below.

D. Talbot Rice, *Byzantine Art* (Pelican 1954); *The Art of Byzantium* (New York 1962 with splendid illustrations); *Art of the Byzantine Era* (London 1963).

O. M. Dalton. *East Christian Art: a survey of the Monuments* (Oxford 1925).

C. Stewart, *Byzantine Legacy* (London 1947). Excellent photographs and a lively introduction to Byzantine art and architecture based on the author's travels.

Early Christian Mosaics, introduction by W. F. Volbach, Iris Colour Book (Batsford 1943); *Byzantine Mosaics*, introduction by P. Meyer, Iris Colour Book (Batsford 1952). Both these have excellent reproductions.

O. Demus, *Byzantine Mosaic Decoration* (2nd ed., London 1953) and *The Mosaics of Norman Sicily* (London 1950).

E. Diez and O. Demus, *Byzantine Mosaics in Greece: Hosios Lucas and Daphni* (Cambridge 1931). With illustrations in colour.

T. Whittemore, *The Mosaics of Haghia Sophia at Instanbul* I–IV (O.U.P. 1933–52); for later reports see *Dumbarton Oaks Papers* IX (1955) onwards.

A. Grabar, *Byzantine Painting* (Skira Series, Geneva 1953). Copious illustrations in colour, including the Balkans and Sicily.

Byzantine Painting, with an introduction and notes by G. Mathew (London 1950). Ten excellent plates in colour, for the most part hitherto unpublished.

Yugoslavia: *Mediaeval Frescoes,* preface by D. Talbot Rice, introduction by S. Radojičć (Unesco World Art Series, New York 1955). Contains some of the best colour reproductions of Serbian frescoes at present available.

Dumbarton Oaks Papers contain valuable reports (with excellent illustrations) on work in progress in Constantinople (notably Hagia Sophia and Kariye Djamii) and elsewhere, as well as studies on more specialised aspects of Byzantine Art.

BYZANTIUM AND ITS NEIGHBOURS

Root of Europe, Studies in the Diffusion of Greek Culture, ed. Michael Huxley (London 1952) is an excellent popular survey by experts, with good illustrations.

D. Obolensky, 'Russia's Byzantine Heritage', *Oxford Slavonic Papers,* vol. I (1950).

N. H. Baynes and Baron Meyendorff, 'The Byzantine Inheritance in Russia', in *Byzantium* (ed. N. H. Baynes and H. St L. B. Moss).

F. Dvornik has written a good deal on the Slav neighbours of Byzantium and their relations with the Eastern Empire. See especially *Les Slaves, Byzance et Rome* (Paris 1926) and *The Making of Central and Eastern Europe* (London 1949). See also *Dumbarton Oaks Papers* XIX (1965)

On relations with Islam see especially *Dumbarton Oaks Papers* XVIII (1964).

On Greek influence in the West see the stimulating studies by D. J. Geanakoplos, *Byzantine East and Latin West: two worlds of Christendom in the Middle Ages and Renaissance. Studies in Ecclesiastical and Cultural History* (Blackwell, Oxford 1966).

In the field of hagiology a difficult but exciting study is that of Paul Peeters, *Le Tréfonds Oriental de l'Hagiographie Byzantine* (Brussels 1950), a brilliant analysis of the interpenetration of Greek and native civilisations with special reference to the saints' lives which took shape in the various lands bordering on the East Mediterranean.

It is perhaps fitting to end this brief survey with a reference to the collected essays of F. Dölger. His *Byzanz und die Europäische Staatenwalt* (Ettal 1953) contains some of his most illuminating studies, as for instance that on the conception of Rome in the thought-world of Byzantium, or those which discuss Byzantine influences in widely differing circles, ranging from the ninth-century Franks to James II of Aragon, admirably demonstrating the nature and extent of Byzantine penetration.

INDEX